P9-DEE-983

A B O R T I O N ' S
S E C O N D
V I C T I M

ABORTION'S
SECOND VICTIM

Pam Koerbel

VICTOR BOOKS™

A DIVISION OF SCRIPTURE PRESS PUBLICATIONS INC.
USA CANADA ENGLAND

Some of the names of persons referred to in this book have been
changed to insure their privacy.

Quotes from *Handbook on Abortion* are used with permission of
Hayes Publishing Company, Inc., Cincinnati, Ohio.

Unless otherwise noted, Scripture quotations are from the *New
American Standard Bible,* © the Lockman Foundation 1960, 1962,
1963, 1968, 1971, 1972, 1973, 1975, 1977. Other quotations are from
the *Holy Bible, New International Version* (NIV), © 1973, 1978, 1984,
International Bible Society, used by permission of Zondervan Bible
Publishers; and the *King James Version* (KJV). Used by permission.

Recommended Dewey Decimal Classification: 301.412
Suggested Subject Heading: SEXUAL ETHICS

Library of Congress Catalog Card Number: 86-60852
ISBN: 0-89693-177-3

Contents

Acknowledgments

A book does not come into being without the encouragement and assistance of many people. I am indebted to the women who shared with me their abortion experiences, often with great personal distress to themselves. Special recognition and thanks are due Bob and Jane Bassett who lovingly cared for my children so I could spend concentrated periods of time researching and writing; Bruce and Cindy Canzanella, Sue Church, Olga Fairfax, and Thea Wagner for their invaluable assistance in critiquing and proofreading the manuscript; and Becky Dodson, for her careful and competent editing and for her patience in guiding me through my first publishing process.

Though words can never express my gratitude, I thank my parents, Carl and Anne Hoffman, who unselfishly gave me life and have unswervingly stood by me; my husband, Leigh, who supported me in every way as I undertook this project during his final year at seminary; and my children, Michael, Mark, and Sarah Anne, for showing me the joy of nurturing new lives.

Though too numerous to name, I thank the many people who encouraged me to "keep on writing" when the task seemed unbearable and impossible; and those who prayed this book into existence, for with prayer this book began and has been completed.

Most of all, I thank my Father, God, to whom I give all the glory.

Introduction

I am not a physician, a pastor, a professional counselor, or a politician. I was at one time, however, a judge and jury of one who condemned an unborn human being to the death penalty. I was also the governor who could have stayed the death sentence, but denied the request. Now I am a wife and mother who is deeply concerned about the mass murders we nicely term *abortions.*

My heart cries out for the children who have been denied their God-given right to live, whether they be whole or broken, bright or slow, rich or poor, wanted or unwanted. And I ache for the women who have received more than they bargained for when they opted for abortion, and who have yet to discover that peace and joy is available to them—that guilt and shame do not have to rule their lives.

Abortion touches more than the baby and its mother. Abortion rends families as fathers, parents, and siblings cry out in unrequited anguish. Friends of the woman, doctors, and nurses—all these are affected in small or great ways.

As I pored over books and articles on abortion, I cried—even after thirteen years—because abortion will always be an emotional subject for me. I cried for my child—untimely, unknown, unborn. I cried for the past he never had, the future he never knew, and the present that I cannot share with him. I cried for myself because I had made a terrible mistake. I say *mistake* because I never realized the enormity of what I was doing until afterward—and then it was too late. I cried because through my own selfishness and confusion, I denied myself an unsurpassed joy and I denied my son the life God intended.

But I pushed away the tears and continued to wade through

7

the volumes of material on this volatile subject. I have heard, seen, and read arguments on both sides of this issue. Having reached the conclusion I was wrong in aborting, I found little help available to assist me to understand why I had aborted, what my actions involved, and how to live in peace with my memories.

What about you? Have you aborted? Are you troubled with guilt, grief, anger, shame, or any other emotions which you didn't expect? Do you wonder why you aren't experiencing the peace of mind which you thought your abortion would provide?

Possibly your emotional reaction to your abortion has been very minor—something you have been able to push into the recesses of your mind with only an occasional twinge of sadness. Or, you may not yet have experienced any negative emotions from your abortion. It may be that until now you have not really considered what abortion is all about, but merely had one and went on with your life. On the other hand, perhaps your abortion has caused emotions so intense that you believe you cannot bear them a moment longer. Whatever your position, *Abortion's Second Victim* has been written for you.

It has been written to help you to understand the truth regarding your abortion and will assist you to understand why emotional problems follow an abortion. Most important, you will discover that you do not have to spend the remainder of your life weighed down with self-recriminations. You can have the peace and joy and freedom you desire. You can pick up the pieces of your life, and once again hold your head high, leaving guilt and shame behind you.

I know this is possible, for I once stood where you stand. Fifteen years ago I consented to an abortion because I believed my actions were just and noble—the best for all concerned. Afterward, I felt some guilt, then self-righteousness, then once again guilt as I began to seriously think about my actions. Now I have found complete forgiveness and peace. So can you.

For some of you about to read this book, abortion lies outside your realm of personal experience. This book will help you understand the mindset and needs of the woman who has aborted and now realizes the enormity of her actions. Since one-fourth of American women of childbearing age have had one or more abortions, the probability is great that you already have a daughter, a sister, a wife, or a friend who has experienced abortion. By reading *Abortion's Second Victim* you will gain insights into the trauma that abortion presents to the woman and you will discover ways in which you can lovingly and beneficially assist her in dealing with her act.

Though the world in general would have us deny significant and lasting emotional reactions following an abortion, the truth is that we do experience an aftermath that for some has lasted for decades. *Abortion's Second Victim* presents us who have aborted as we rarely permit the world to see us—hurting, ashamed, and wanting desperately to be forgiven and accepted. Heeding the advice and wishes of government, pro-choice groups, friends, and family, American women have consented to become unwitting victims in the tragedy that is abortion. You see, abortion is more than taking the life of an unborn human being—abortion is an act which forever alters the life of the woman who submits to an abortion.

As part of my research for this book, I compiled a questionnaire which forty-six women completed. Their responses to my questions are cited and evaluated throughout this book.

It is my earnest prayer that if you have never had an abortion, this book will help you to better understand those of us who have lived through one; if by any chance you are presently considering an abortion, I pray you will clearly see that abortion will not be the easy way out of the difficult situation in which you find yourself; and finally, if you have experienced an abortion, hold fast to the truth that although you can never retrieve that moment in time, there is hope. And as your wounds heal—and they *can* heal—I pray you will courageously seek opportunities to comfort other women who have allowed themselves to become victims of our age.

When you have finished reading this book, please write to me and tell me how it has affected you.

PAM KOERBEL
3718 HARMON AVENUE
LANDOVER HILLS, MD 20784

*Beware lest any man spoil you
through philosophy and vain deceit,
after the tradition of men,
after the rudiments of the world,
and not after Christ*

(Colossians 2:8, κjv).

To Leigh

Who lovingly shared the weight
of my burden until I learned
to lay it down.

PART ONE

ANATOMY OF AN ABORTION

O N E

Freedom to Choose

I remember clearly that crisp, sunny November morning when my world was turned upside down. As I dropped the coins one by one into the pay phone to place the call, I was pensive. Ten o'clock—the time Dr. Rosen had asked me to call.

The wait had been almost unbearable since the test was done. Three days . . . the phone rang once, twice—then the nurse answered, "Dr. Rosen's office."

"May I speak with Dr. Rosen, please?" My palms were sweating as I waited for Dr. Rosen to come on the line.

"Dr. Rosen speaking."

"This is Pam Hoffman calling to get the results of my pregnancy test," I whispered into the receiver. As I spoke a nearby voice startled me. Quickly I glanced over my shoulder to see who was listening, but the sound came from behind a closed door. No one had heard me.

"The test was positive," Dr. Rosen responded to my inquiry about my pregnancy test.

"Positive! Are you sure? There is no mistake?"

"There is no mistake, Pam. You are about eight weeks pregnant."

"Thank you, doctor. I'll stop in to see you as soon as I can get home. Good-bye," I said as I hung up the phone.

For a brief moment, I was sorry. Then as swiftly my worries turned to joy. Emotions exploded inside of me—wonder, excitement, and anticipation at the thought of the new life growing inside of me. I felt an urgent need to share my news with someone.

I raced to my college dormitory and went straight to my best friend. "Lisa! I'm going to be a mother!"

I was so excited that it wasn't until I'd flopped onto the bed that my mind registered the look on Lisa's face.

"Oh, Pam, that's *terrible*." Lisa spoke with such candor that the wind was momentarily knocked out of my sails.

Lisa and I talked briefly. She agreed to keep my secret until I decided what I would do.

Then I went to my room and sat down to think. At that moment the awful reality of being single and pregnant crushed my spirits. What should I do?

Reflections
My thoughts drifted back over my life. The oldest of four children, I was raised in a Christian home and attended church from infancy. As a teenager, I participated in youth group activities, taught Sunday School, and edited the church paper.

I knew about Christ's death and resurrection, but I didn't know Him personally. I had a Bible, but never bothered to read it.

My parents, trying to compensate for the impoverished and strict upbringing they had had, were indulgent and far too lenient with me. They taught me how to live and then expected me to fulfill the trust they placed in me. I had no curfew and never had to answer for where I had been or with whom. My parents just expected me to do the right thing.

On the surface I was shy and quiet, but inside I desired to be part of the "in" crowd. As a teen I moved further and further from God, finally setting Him aside completely. For acceptance, I allowed others to dictate my actions, though I was searching for something I never quite found.

Then I met Tim. People were drawn to Tim's charismatic personality and accepted me because of my association with him. Though he was engaged to another girl, Tim and I dated for more than two years.

I believed virginity was the most precious possession a woman could give her bridegroom, and I kept it until I was almost twenty-two. But I wanted Tim to love *me*, to marry *me*. When I finally gave in, he reminded me afterward that we were only casually dating. There were to be no strings attached to our relationship. We soon parted ways.

Six months later I started my junior year of college, determined to straighten out my life. Then Tim invited me over to his apartment for dinner. Foolishly, I accepted.

One thing led to another and I can remember afterward saying half-jokingly, "You know, Tim, I *could* be pregnant."

"How could you be pregnant? You're still on the pill, aren't you?" Tim's voice betrayed a touch of fear.

"No, I went off six months ago when we stopped dating. There's never been anyone but you, and so I figured why continue to take them."

"Are you crazy? Why didn't you *tell* me?" Tim sputtered.

"I never expected things to go this far. What if I *am* pregnant? What would you do?"

Then Tim relaxed at the thought of this one time episode leading to pregnancy and said with a twinkle in his eye, "If you are, then I'll marry you."

We saw each other only in classes after that, each of us going our own direction.

But now, when he finds out he's going to be a father, everything will be OK, I thought. *He wil love the baby as I do, I just know it, and he will want to marry me.*

"Pam, phone for you," interrupted my thoughts.

Betrayed!

Overwhelmed by the burden of my secret, Lisa had called my parents and told them I had something urgent to tell them. When Mom phoned, she had already guessed my news.

As I explained, she listened and loved me. We had always had an open relationship and I probably would have shared this with her sooner or later. Still, Lisa had betrayed me! *My parents shouldn't have found out like this! They're probably sitting at home right now, worrying, suffering, praying. Betrayed!* I wondered who else Lisa would tell.

The next morning I saw Tim heading toward the campus library. I ran toward him. "Tim, we have to talk."

Fear stood out on Tim's face as I spoke, indicating he already knew what I was about to say. "Don't blame *me*," he glowered. "I had *nothing* to do with this! You can't prove a thing!"

Stunned, I pleaded, "Can't we please talk about this?"

"No." And he walked away.

Friday afternoon I headed for home. As I walked through the front door, I saw disappointment mixed with love on my parents' faces. My parents are practical people and, hiding the shame they must have felt, let me know that they wanted me to have and keep the baby, their first grandchild.

We sat down to discuss my options: have the child and raise it myself, put it up for adoption, or get an abortion.

The option to abort became available in July 1970, when New York passed an abortion-on-demand law that rocked the nation. A woman was now free to choose her unborn child's destiny through the twenty-fourth week of pregnancy.

But in the early stages of my pregnancy, I never seriously considered abortion as an option. My parents thought it was wrong—and so did I.

To many, adoption is the honorable solution. It circumvents abortion and frees the mother from an unwanted or untimely involvement with her child.

Fifteen years ago I briefly considered putting my baby up for adoption. But I realized I could not carry a child nine months and then give him away, never to see him again. How could I bear to live my life peering into the face of every unknown child and wondering, *Is he mine?*

My doctor advised me to consider a private adoption. He knew of couples who desperately wanted children and would pay all my medical expenses if I would sign the infant over to them. I could even see the baby before I gave him up. But I kept thinking, *Why should someone else have the joy of raising my child? I can't do it—I just can't do it!* No, adoption was out also.

Fiercely independent, I thought I could manage caring for my child and deluded myself into thinking everything was all right. Regardless of what neighbors and friends thought, I intended to live and raise my child in my parents' home. Unworried about the future, I returned to school, determined to continue classes through the fall semester.

To my dismay, during my two day absence the college grapevine had spread its juicy news. Tim publicly denied he was the father, recruiting friends to lie for him and say they'd had sexual relations with me, thereby negating any chance for my winning a paternity suit.

I talked freely about my approaching motherhood, always positively, needing desperately to talk this out, to be accepted, to have someone say, "You're doing the right thing." But no one did.

One friend explained that the "thing" inside of me was nothing more than a parasite, living off me, using me . . . just a parasite, nothing more. She encouraged me to get rid of it. *But I don't want to get rid of it. Why can't people understand? Why?*

Mom and Dad and I talked again and Mom brought reality into sharp focus by saying, "You know, Pam, you will have to drop out of school to care for this baby. I work full-time and it will be your responsibility. You can't expect Dad and me to raise it for you."

I had never considered what my future would be like *after* the baby was born. *All my dreams and plans gone? No! Never!* I panicked and began to consider abortion.

Not once did I envision a little boy holding my hand, learning to walk and looking up and saying, "I love you, Mommy." It never occurred to me I was merely a vessel privileged to shelter a growing being, preparing to take its place in the world. I never considered anyone but myself.

Three months pregnant, I registered at a New York hospital clinic for prenatal care. The fetus was growing normally; everything looked fine. My social worker, Mrs. Lucas, urged me to have my baby, and then if I felt the burden too great, to put it up for adoption. She told me that I might not feel anything now, but that later I would one day regret having had an abortion. But I reasoned, *If I can't keep my baby, no one else will have it either.*

How I hated that clinic! Though it was bitterly cold outside, the clinic was hot and stuffy and cramped with Spanish-speaking men, women, and children from New York's poorest section. I kept my appointments as scheduled because I wanted to make sure my baby was doing OK. Looking back, I can see the incongruity of being worried about a child I contemplated killing.

Doubts

By January, I had to make a decision. Time was running out. Soon it would be too late. Until then, carrying a baby was an abstract fact, but by January I was beginning to show. I felt the baby move and knew it was alive. The fact that I really was pregnant hit me.

Friends began to avoid me, talking behind my back and observing me from a distance. The true friendship I needed was gone.

Shamelessly I moved through campus, proud of the life inside of me and scared of the future. I asked my friends, professors, and even God for advice. I reasoned with myself. How I wish I had taken my dusty old Bible off the shelf and read what God had to say, but I didn't, perhaps because I already knew. It was not, "Thy will be done," but *mine.*

I knew one of the professors in the biology department and went to him with my problem, thinking he would be able to advise me.

"It's an unfortunate thing that has happened to you, Pam. However, you must realize that life begins at birth. True, what you are carrying has a potential for life, but it isn't alive yet. Not as *we* know life. You mustn't be too hard on yourself."

"But it moved," I argued.

"Yes, but muscular reactions occur before life as well as after death. Don't be alarmed about it."

That makes sense, I told myself. *But can I believe it? Is it true?*

Finally, Tim agreed to talk to me. As we began to talk, I realized he was as afraid as I was; two grown children deciding on the fate of their unborn child.

"It's our baby. All right, it was a mistake—but it's *our baby!* I want to keep it. Tim, all I want from you is support for the baby and for it to have your name. Nothing else." I fought back the tears.

"Are you crazy? I'm not even sure it's mine!" Tim exploded at my suggestion.

I could feel my heart break at the realization that this man definitely did not love me or our baby. But I still loved Tim and was willing to try anything to gain his love. So I said, "If you really want me to have an abortion, I will. I'll get rid of our baby if it makes you happy."

"That's what I want," he said.

Fighting for a reason to avoid the abortion, I announced, "Then you'll have to pay for it. I'm broke."

"Why should I?"

"Then I'll keep it." I had Tim in a corner.

"I'll pay half."

"I don't have *any* money!" I screamed.

"OK, OK—I'll pay the whole shot. But you'll owe me half as soon as you can get the money together. You'll have to sign an I.O.U."

After our talk I made an appointment for the abortion. Three weeks to wait because of all the women invading New York from across the country to rid themselves of their little "burdens." Three more weeks to wait in hopeless indecision.

I can honestly say that had a legal abortion been unavailable to me, my son would be alive today. I would never have considered an illegal abortion because the backstreet clinics were too risky. After all, wasn't that one of the major reasons to legalize abortion—for the safety of the mother?

As the day drew closer, I still had serious doubts. I really *wanted* the baby, but the opposing desire to be free was pulling me to shreds. In desperation, I visited the college chaplain. Surely this man of God would steer me in the right direction and set my mind at ease.

Steve told me my mind and body were given to me by God and that I had control over them. These things happened and God understood. Steve said he would assist me in any way he could, but the decision was ultimately mine. And he said I shouldn't feel guilty. Times had changed. I didn't have to bring a child that would be unwanted and unloved into the world. If abortion was the right thing for me, then it was OK.

Steve wished me God's blessings. I left his office and met the baby's father. In silence we drove to the hospital.

Tears rolled down my cheeks as Tim escorted me inside. To the right was a small, stuffy admittance room. February 13, 1971, one o'clock. We were right on time. We stepped up to the window. The paperwork was waiting and Tim paid the bill.

"Remember, you owe me half when you get the money."

"I'll remember."

"Well, see you kid."

Choosing to Be Free

Ten minutes later my name was called. I picked up my small blue overnight case and looked at the wheelchair the attendant pushed toward me.

"Do I have to use that?"

"Yes, please sit down."

"But I'm not sick. I'd rather walk."

"Sorry. Regulations—you have to ride."

We exited the elevator on the OB/GYN floor. To the right was the wing where women went to give birth. We headed to the left wing which housed all the women with other "female ailments."

I was placed in a ward with twenty-three other women. Privacy was provided by a thin muslin curtain hanging on rings over a metal rod that could be pulled around three sides of my bed.

Horrified at the poverty, lack of privacy, and noise, I sat on my bed and looked around the ward. Directly to my left was a young Spanish woman who had been induced the day before. She was waiting to expel the fetus. She spoke no English. To my right was a black woman in her middle thirties who had had a hysterectomy and would never bear the children she wanted. I can still see the sorrow in her eyes when I told her why I was there.

In order to isolate myself, I read, speaking only to nurses and to the woman on my right, who tried to strike up an acquaintance with me.

My social worker arrived. "How are you, Pam? Is everything OK?" Then she spoke softly and asked, "Are you sure you want to go through with this?"

"Yes, it's the only way."

"We discussed that. You still have other options."

"No, I don't. The father doesn't want the baby. This is it." I was here because Tim wanted me here. Always I had managed to blame someone else for my failings or wrongdoings. An expert at deception, I had reached the point where I could even deceive myself.

Somehow, I slept that night. The next morning the college chaplain stopped by to talk. I expressed my doubts about what I was doing.

"Do you really think it's OK? I mean, isn't it like murder?"

Steve assured me that it would be a greater wrong to bring a child into a world where he was not wanted. This was best for the baby and me. There was no need to feel guilty. Steve prayed for me to have peace.

Steve is right, I reasoned. *It's my body, my life. To be burdened with a child now would be foolish. Tim doesn't want the baby either. There's no need to feel guilty.*

Steve left and I waited, digging my nose into my book to avoid thinking.

Someone called my name. I looked at my watch—2:15 in the afternoon. It was February 14, 1971, Valentine's Day. I was led into a small brightly lit room at the end of the ward. The door closed.

Until that moment, abortion was just an awful word I read about in newspapers—something that happened to *other* people. Now the word became reality. I was going to willfully abort my unborn child.

I screamed, "No! *No!* Please stop! I *want* my baby!" I began sobbing hysterically.

"Nurse, calm her down. We're wasting time," the doctor said.

Turning to me, he said, "Look, honey—if you want to go through with this, it *has* to be today. Make up your mind. Once you leave this room, that's it. What will it be?"

What should I do?

I felt as though I was the only woman ever to be indecisive about having an abortion. Approaching my twenty-fourth week—the legal limit for abortion—I *had* to decide. Next week would be too late.

"It will all be over in fifteen minutes—a very simple procedure," the doctor continued. "But we can't go ahead without your verbal consent. We're not going to force you. What's it going to be?" He sounded impatient.

I really wanted this baby. Wasn't that why I'd put off this decision for almost six months? But I wanted to finish my education and live my life and not be burdened with a child. No more deliberating. The months had rushed to this moment. No changing my mind. It was now or never.

Knowing the wrong I was about to do, but numb with fear, I said, "OK, go ahead."

As the doctor worked, he explained the procedure to me. "This will tingle just a little. After that, all you will feel is pressure."

He injected novacaine to anesthetize my abdominal area. The pain was excruciating. I squeezed the nurse's hand and held my breath.

This is best for me and my baby.

Then the largest needle I had ever seen was inserted below my navel directly into the womb. I felt a strong pressure as the needle went in. Fascinated, I watched as though I was a spectator.

"We are removing one-half pint of amniotic fluid and replacing it with an equal amount of saline—a strong salt solution."

I saw a yellowish liquid come out. Then, as the saline was injected, I cried out, "I feel movement inside! What's happening?" I was alarmed. The turbulence was forceful.

"Nothing to worry about. It's only the fluid being injected. We're almost done."

The needle was removed. My belly was washed and a bandage was placed over the tiny hole left from the needle. An IV was inserted in my left hand.

"What's that for? I thought I was all done."

"Standard procedure, in case of complications."

"What kind of complications?"

"Nothing to worry about." The nurse smiled at me.

The doctor looked at me. "Now you just have to wait. The fetus will expel itself in approximately twenty-four hours—sometimes a little less, sometimes a little more. You can expect some pain because you are delivering a dead baby—rather, a dead fetus— and you must do all the work during labor. Call the nurse if you need pain medication."

The entire procedure had taken less than half an hour. I walked back to my bed, greeted sadly and solemnly by Mrs. Lucas. She pointed across the room to a fifteen-year-old girl who had come to be aborted. My social worker asked me if I would talk to her.

I told the young girl to have her baby, to raise the child, and to love it. Then I explained the abortion procedure. I also told her it was wrong to have a sexual relationship outside of marriage, but a second mistake never covers up the first. The girl went home, determined to have her baby. How I wished I could have turned back the hands of time, but for my baby it was too late.

Hours passed. The Spanish woman was released, but then readmitted around midnight in bad shape. Bearing twins, she had aborted only one. The doctors hadn't realized she had another baby inside of her.

My pains began to come. The pressure was tremendous—it *is* more difficult to deliver a dead child than a living one. I took as many Darvons as the nurses would allow. I had no privacy except the curtain pulled around my bed. Drenched with sweat, I writhed in silent misery. Suddenly, it was over.

Mustering my strength, I buzzed for a nurse. A gentle, quiet woman assisted me, surprised I hadn't cried out in agony.

"It's visiting hours," I whispered. "I didn't want anyone to know." It was such a private act to have to accomplish in such a public place.

Examining the baby she said, "Oh, look—it's a little boy."

In my semi-drugged condition, I propped myself up and, without thinking, looked down between my legs. There lay a perfectly formed little person—a boy. His reddish-blue body was curled in the classic fetal position. Hair and facial details weren't there yet, but I remember staring at his perfectly formed tiny fingers and toes. Seeing his frail body brought the reality of my actions into sharp focus. Totally dependent on me to sustain his life, I had failed him. I had murdered my own child!

"Oh, good, the placenta is intact," the nurse stated matter-of-factly as she examined the tissue. "Everything will be OK now. I'll clean you up and you can rest."

I asked about burial and the nurse told me if a fetus weighed a pound or more it was issued a death certificate and buried. She weighed the baby. Small for his age, he weighed only eleven ounces. I listened as they flushed him down the huge disposal like a piece of garbage.

My son.

I called out to God in anguish, but He couldn't comfort me because I didn't know Him. I turned my face to my pillow and silently mourned.

Complications

The next morning I passed a solid piece of tissue. Horrified, I told the nurses I thought I'd passed a piece of placenta.

"How would you know?" they challenged me.

Because I insisted, I was examined, this time by a woman doctor. She was rough in her manner and speech. "You're OK; you can go home today," she told me.

The hospital released me. Prior to leaving, I passed another piece of placenta. This time instead of flushing it, I carried it to the nurses' station.

"What do you call this?" I demanded, filled with fear.

I was scheduled for a D & C to remove the remaining placenta. The tissue had to be removed.

Food was withheld for twenty-four hours. Then a nurse prepped me for surgery. An orderly wheeled me down the corridor to an operating room. I was transferred from the gurney to the table.

The room looked so much smaller than I had expected. Everything seemed so close together . . . things were beginning to blur. . . .

"How long will this take?" I mumbled.

"Not long."

An IV was inserted and the anesthesiologist asked me, "What is your name?"

"Pamela Jean Hoffman."

He placed a mask over my face and the room faded away.

I awoke in the recovery room. Things were fuzzy, but a kind voice said, "Hi, everything is fine."

But was it? I had an irrational fear that somehow they had sterilized me. Would I ever be able to have another child? Fear gripped me in its icy fingers.

After I recovered from the D & C, a member of the hospital staff instructed me in the use of birth control pills and gave me a three-month supply. No one mentioned abstinence as an option to unwanted pregnancy.

Seven days after entering the hospital, I walked out into the bright sunshine of a cold February day. My problem was gone and I was healthy and free to resume my life.

The Price of Freedom

I stepped back onto campus and into the mainstream of college life without as much hoopla as I had anticipated. It almost seemed as if my friends breathed a united sigh of relief—Pam's little episode was over.

My social life "improved" following my abortion. Men who never before had given me a second look began to ask me out. I soon learned they invited me out with one thought in mind.

One guy picked me up at the dorm and took me directly to a necking spot near campus and, when I refused his advances, sneered, "Aw, come on—everyone knows about you."

Indeed a lot of men thought they knew about me for Tim had done his task well in spreading the word that "Pam slept around." Still I felt no animosity toward Tim. In my eyes, he could do no wrong.

While my abortion was an "open secret" on campus, outside of college only members of my immediate family knew. I realized Mom and Dad were really upset over what I had done, but we never discussed it. They just looked a little sadder and older and my dad didn't look me in the eye for a long time. My sister and brothers have never mentioned abortion to me—ever.

I sometimes wondered what the neighbors thought when they saw me suddenly unpregnant, but I wasn't living at home and didn't have to face them as my parents did. It wasn't any concern of mine—I was free and that's all that mattered.

My sense of euphoria didn't last long. Alone at night I had hours to think about what I had done. I tortured myself with thoughts of my dead baby. I mourned the child I had destroyed.

I resumed taking tranquilizers in order to sleep at night and amphetamines to stay alert during the day. I had given up taking pills when I became pregnant—for the sake of my baby. Now none of it mattered.

Life around me continued at its frantic pace, unaware of one lonely person crying in confusion and guilt. *Why do I feel this way? Everyone said it was OK, not to worry, it was best for all concerned.*

I soon became bitter and resentful. Everywhere I went I saw pregnant women and mothers holding infants. Posters declaring the horror of abortion condemned my actions and news articles proclaiming the rights of women to rule their own bodies leaped off the pages in self-righteous conspiracy. I began to justify my actions.

How could anyone say whether an abortion was right or wrong unless they had been through one? What did anyone know of the torment involved in deciding to sacrifice a baby? How could people take sides on this issue?

I began a campaign of self-righteous pity. After all, I reasoned, I had just lost my first child. I had given him up because the father had asked me to and somewhere in the back of my mind I reasoned that at last I had proved my love for Tim. My parents had actually expected me to give up school to care for the baby—if they wanted him, why hadn't they offered to care for him? God should never have let me get pregnant in the first place. Oh, yes, it was *so* easy to cast blame. The more I thought about it, the more convinced I became that what I had done was right.

I guess the Lord wrote the first chapter of Romans just for me. I knew God and chose not to glorify Him because *my* way was better. He handed me over to my own desires and I continued to worship the world. I had sinned and now sanctioned it.

God could have brushed me aside, but instead He began working in my life even before I asked for help. One month after my abortion, God brought a wonderful caring man into my life.

Leigh had taken me to a fraternity Christmas party when I had been pregnant. His friendship was one I valued because he made no demands and did not condemn me. We started dating and enjoyed each other's company.

Summer came and Leigh and I continued to date regularly. He offered me his fraternity pin, but I hesitated. I still loved Tim and I considered Leigh only a good friend. But Leigh loved me and wanted a more permanent relationship. I took the pin, feeling guilty but somehow secure for the first time in my life.

I started my senior year as Leigh's pinmate. When time came for the fraternity to choose its sweetheart, friends actually campaigned for me to win. It was then I found out that many of Leigh's fraternity brothers and their girls felt I had gotten a raw deal from Tim. They chose me to be sweetheart to help compensate in some way for the way they had treated me. Though it was too late, I was deeply touched to think people really cared about me.

Abortion was far from my mind during that busy senior year as I finished up course work and made plans for my marriage to Leigh.

Leigh and I were married the September following graduation. But I still loved Tim and vowed never to have children by another man. Though I was on the pill, I feared pregnancy to such an extent that Leigh and I rarely had sexual relations after the first few months of our marriage.

Without meaning to, I had surrounded myself with impenetrable walls. I was not at peace, but was able to live with myself without feeling guilty about the abortion. I did this by simply refusing to think about what I had done—I closed it out of my mind. I was depressed much of the time and suffered a nervous breakdown within six months of our marriage. Leigh stood by me, like a rock, there when I needed to talk or to cry. But I never mentioned my abortion to him—nor to anyone else for a long time.

Following my breakdown we moved to another part of New York State. Leigh's parents lived near us and didn't know about my past. Suddenly, I was faced with keeping my abortion a secret. It had been one thing to live with the knowledge that those around me knew and more or less accepted me. It was quite another thing knowing that no one knew and wondering what they would think if they did know. I found it hard to keep silent when the topic of abortion came up for discussion. I wondered if my silence or facial expressions were obvious.

In 1974 I begged my obstetrician to sterilize me. I knew our limited sex life was hurting Leigh and I intended to remedy that by eliminating the possibility of having children. But my doctor refused.

Then there were the nightmares. For many years I dreamed of babies being flushed down drains and fetuses pickled in jars. Discussing abortion sickened me, yet I had become obsessed with the subject.

Guilt consumed me as I began to understand why I had aborted and what I had done to myself, my baby, and others around me. I would never be convicted for my crime. That didn't matter—for I had sentenced myself to a lifetime of guilt and depression.

Two years had passed since I had heard from Tim. Leigh knew how I felt about Tim and accepted this as something he could not change. Then one day Tim called, explaining he was in the area visiting with friends. When he asked if he could come over, Leigh graciously said, "Yes."

When Tim arrived, my heart beat a little faster. I still cared for this man and there was nothing I could do to deny it. But I knew Tim's feelings for me were based on friendship, and it was as a friend he visited us.

"I just wanted to see how you two were doing. I thought I'd better wish you a belated congratulations on your wedding."

Then Tim handed me the I.O.U. I had signed so long ago and said, "Consider this a belated gift."

Tim's gift was generous and offered in all sincerity, but my mind went reeling back to the night we had agreed to split the $260 fee that was to set us free from a reality we had refused to face. At the time, it had seemed a large sum to pay and I had never thrown in my promised share. Now Tim had given me a $130 gift—my half of the bill.

Tim *was* free and never realized the money he paid for my abortion constituted only a small part of the total price. I was still paying every day of my life—not in hard, cold cash—but in diminished self-respect and mental torment. The $260 had failed to set *me* free. My abortion had been only the beginning of a private hell that taunted my waking hours and disturbed my sleep.

Somehow the years passed by without my much realizing it. Ours wasn't much of a marriage and I knew all the blame rested on me. Leigh and I moved several times, each time taking my secret with us. I needed desperately to talk to someone who understood . . . someone who had been through an abortion also. But there was no one.

I kept it all inside me, festering like the untreated wound that it was.

TWO

Taking the Cure

Despite my topsy-turvy emotional life, I had developed a career which was both satisfying and held opportunity for advancement. I was manager of a small shop which specialized in yarn and needlecrafts. Responsibility for five employees and a large inventory rested solely with me.

I gave that job my all—spending extra hours, days and nights, working to build sales. I brought work home and traveled when the need arose. I wasn't conscious of it at the time, but it helped me avoid the personal problems I did not know how to resolve.

Then, in the winter of 1975, two smiling, soft-spoken women entered the store. They asked if I would talk about crafts at the next meeting of the Christian Business and Professional Women's Council. I was eager to promote the store, and the prospect of spending an evening with other Christian women (of which I considered myself to be one) was manna to my hungry soul. I had not attended church regularly for several years, but having spent my entire youth immersed in church activities and the fellowship they offered, I felt a void caused by the lack of what I considered spiritual fulfillment. Delightedly, I accepted their invitation.

Polly, one of the women who had approached me about speaking, called me a couple of times before the meeting with words of encouragement. She also offered to drive me to the meeting so I wouldn't feel awkward walking in all alone.

It was cold and pouring rain as we arrived at the meeting. In contrast to the dismal outdoors, warmth and bright lights greeted us as we entered the banquet room. I listened to the happy chatter and gentle laughter of over a hundred women as they settled down to an evening of meaningful relaxation.

As I spoke that January evening in 1976, I wondered if anyone could see or hear my knees knocking. I had never spoken before a large group. To make matters worse, I was using a microphone for the first time. My voice startled me as it blared out over the speakers. The presentation was stilted, neither witty nor original, but the women heartily applauded my efforts. With hands visibly shaking, I took my seat.

In order to calm myself, I listened intently to the main speaker. I do not recall her name, but I remember clearly her words. She spoke on Revelation 3:20, "Behold, I (Christ) stand at the door and knock; if anyone hears My voice and opens the door, I will come in to him, and will dine with him, and he with Me." That precious woman said some things I had not listened to previously. Oh, I had heard similar words, but I had never really *listened.* This is what she said:

In my hands I hold a key—the key to my heart and life. Christ, who so lovingly died for my sins, wants to enter my heart and live there, cleansing me from my sins and thereby granting me eternal life with God in heaven one day. However, Christ is a gentleman. Though He wants to forgive my sins, He will never force His way into my life. The decision has to be mine and mine alone. Christ stands outside the door of my heart and knocks, patiently and lovingly waiting for me to say "please come in." The door of my heart is locked and can be opened only from the inside; I hold the only key. I alone can open the door and let Jesus Christ into my heart so that He may forgive my sins and begin a new life in me.

As the speaker concluded her message, she asked, "Will you unlock the door of your heart to Jesus and invite Him in?"

In one startling moment I realized that I was not a Christian, had never been a Christian, and could only become a Christian by personally accepting Christ's cleansing of sins. I didn't understand how or even why He would want to do such a wondrous work in a vile sinner like me. Yet, I believed God's words in Revelation 3:20. At that moment, I bowed my head and asked Christ into my heart and life as my personal Saviour from my sins.

On the way home from the meeting, I confided to Polly, "I accepted Christ this evening."

"Oh, Pam, that's wonderful! I'm so happy for you. You won't believe the wonderful things God has in store for your life now that you belong to Him."

"But Polly, I always thought I *was* a Christian. I have always believed in Christ."

"You know, Pam, that's where so many people are mistaken. John 1:12 tells us that 'As many as *received* Him, to *them* He gave the right to become children of God, even to those who believe on His name.' Salvation is a very personal experience. Each of us must receive Christ individually. Though He died for everyone, the decision to accept His death for our personal sins is our own choice. You made that choice tonight."

"I know. It's different than before. I am so filled with peace right now that I don't know how to explain it," I said through happy tears.

Polly grabbed my hand and softly said, "I understand."

As she dropped me off at home, Polly suggested we meet for coffee one morning soon and talk some more. Happily I agreed.

"How was your evening?" Leigh asked me as I opened the door.

"OK."

I wonder if he can see the glow on my face? I'm not going to let him burst my bubble—this is my secret and I'm not sharing it with Leigh. He has never wanted anything to do with God, and if I don't tell him he'll never have an opportunity to laugh at me!

We went to bed that night together, and yet so alone. I had found something that, unknown to me, had changed the course of my life. Leigh was still searching and I wasn't even willing to help him.

Changes
In March I was passed up for a promotion. Bitter over the realization that someone younger, less educated, and less experienced than I had gotten the promotion, I talked with my boss. She patiently explained that moving up the career ladder meant more than just increasing sales.

So I worked harder. My results were excellent, but my methods were lousy. My staff must have been saints to put up with my dictatorial ways. I was hard and cold—a machine disguised in human flesh—working at my job without taking into consideration that my employees were people with feelings as well as needs to be met. To the customers I was polite, but curt, meeting their requests but doing only what was required.

Polly and I met several times and talked about Christ. I had always been a religious person, desiring to know more about God, and Polly was the first person I'd met who had real answers to my many questions. But I never saw Christ as the solution to the problems I was having with people because I did not realize I was having any problems. Oblivious to all except myself and my own needs, I continued to live in a world of isolation.

By sheer force of willpower on my part (and undoubtedly a lot of kindness to the customers by my employees), my store increased steadily in sales. In July my boss offered me a transfer to a larger store in the chain. Located several hours away, it would mean moving. At that time, Leigh was teaching music at a local school. We discussed my opportunity for advancement and decided that if Leigh could find full-time employment in three days, I would accept the transfer.

Though I steadily ignored Him, God was working in our lives. Leigh got his job—working for a trucking firm (a second occupation for which he had trained) within two hours of beginning to seek employment! Within a week we were relocated in upper New York State.

Dedicated to my job, I pushed my staff at the new location harder than ever. Sales began to rise, but the employee turnover was frequent. I just couldn't understand what I was doing wrong.

My personal life wasn't exactly running smoothly either. Leigh and I lived together, but went our separate ways. We communicated on the surface only. I continually threatened to leave Leigh because I still loved Tim. I really wanted to go, but never did, perhaps realizing deep in my subconscious that no one would ever care for me as Leigh did.

In January 1977, I awoke in the middle of the night to discover Leigh gone from our bed. I lay there wondering where he was. *He's left me! What will I do? I didn't mean all those things I said about not loving him, but it was my way of avenging the hurt inside of me.*

Some time later Leigh quietly slipped into bed. Touching my shoulder he asked, "Pam, are you awake?"

"Yes, where have you been?"

"Pam, I've just accepted Christ as my personal Saviour," Leigh whispered in a choked voice.

Tears streamed down my face. I turned to Leigh and hugged

him as I said, "Oh, Leigh, I'm so happy." He told me how he had been led to a saving knowledge of Jesus Christ over the past several months by an employee at work and I told him of my conversion a year previously. Something special had happened to our lives and we both knew it.

Leigh had attended a Bible church for two Sundays and now he said, "I want *you* to come to church with me this Sunday."

Having been a Lutheran all of my life, I wasn't too keen on switching denominations. But Leigh, in his gentle, yet persuasive way, got me to agree to attend church with him.

That Sunday I heard the Bible taught in all its fullness and accuracy. We went the following Sunday, and the next, and the next. I missed the ritual and strict format of the Lutheran church, but realized this Bible church offered something most churches didn't. The emptiness within me was filled as I hungrily fed on the Word of God.

God had placed us in a church filled with vibrant, mature Christians eager to assist spiritual babies such as ourselves. We began to mature in our faith, little by little appropriating into our lives the truths of Scripture.

I remember when we decided to begin tithing. We had never given more than a dollar or two each Sunday. Now we realized the responsibility of each believer to give willingly on a regular basis to support the work of the local church which fed us the Word of God so faithfully. But we were strapped up to our necks with debts—from four years of college, from buying on credit, three cars, and all those miscellaneous things we "had" to have. There was not a single extra penny for giving to God. Why, we were barely scraping by as it was!

"Well," Leigh said one day, "we're going to have to do this by faith." That next Sunday we gave 10 percent of Leigh's take-home pay (we weren't yet willing to trust God enough to give Him 10 percent of the gross!). Mathematically we've never been able to figure it out on paper, but as we faithfully gave to the Lord each week, we always had enough—just enough—to meet each and every bill! We were seeing in practice that God honors His Word and our obedience to it.

I also began to understand God's desire to change people who were willing to trust Him to work in their lives. When I came to know Christ as my personal Saviour, Leigh and I had been married four years. During that time I was faithful to my husband physically, but not mentally. Many times I angrily told Leigh that I loved Tim and not him. Though I rarely saw Tim, I thought about him constantly. On those occasions when our paths did cross, my heart pounded in my chest at the sight of Tim.

Finally, I yielded to God in this area of my life, but not without a struggle. Often, thoughts of Tim would come slithering into my mind unbeckoned. At those times I would consciously remember that Satan wanted me to have these wrong thoughts but that "I can do all things through Christ which strengthens me" (Phil. 4:13). The last time I saw Tim was in 1978, and I realized God had answered my prayer to remove all my emotions regarding him. As I looked at Tim no bells rang; my heart beat normally. I was *really* free! I had had a taste of victory over a problem that nearly ruined my marriage, and with God's help, I was going to win the war!

However, there was one particular area in which I was not about to yield myself to God. I did not want children. I hated them! I blamed my feelings on my abortion, using that as justification for refusing to obey God.

A Lesson to Learn
I had grown enough in my Christian life to know that God wanted me to have children and that I was now consciously fighting Him all the way. Because God loved me so much, He took drastic action to get my attention.

Once a week, deliveries of new merchandise arrived at the store. It was part of my job to unpack these cartons. Some of the boxes weighed more than 85 pounds. Filled with yarn, they were approximately four feet high by two and a half feet square in width. In order for a woman to move these monsters, it was necessary to grab them around the top and turn them on a bottom corner to "walk" them across the floor. One morning as I moved one of these large cartons, I felt a stabbing pain in my side that ran down my right leg. Ignoring the pain, I continued to unload the merchandise. The next day I was in pain. It continued to worsen and I knew I'd damaged my back. I filed an injury statement, but continued working because I was short-handed.

Though injured in February, it was April when I finally took my doctor's advice and requested sick time. Physical therapy wasn't helping and my neurosurgeon wanted to operate. But I was not at peace about exploratory surgery that might find nothing and leave me with permanent scar tissue on my back. In desperation I skeptically consulted a chiropractor. Through total bed rest and regular treatments, my back began to heal. Although unknown to me at the time, I was to remain bedridden for nearly a year.

My injury was covered under Workmen's Compensation, but our income had been cut by more than 25 percent. We continued to give regularly to our local church. God was testing us and we were succeeding, at least in this area of faith. It's interesting that we could be so faithful to obey God in some areas and yet remain hardened to His will in others.

Once again Leigh proved his love for me by taking over the housework. He vacuumed, dusted, cooked, and laundered our clothes in a spirit of joyful servanthood. To keep my mind occupied during the long, lonesome daytime hours when Leigh was at work, I decided to read through my Bible.

I began reading at Genesis and read every word to the end of Revelation. My prayer life was at a peak during this time and I usually spent an hour or more each day on my knees in prayer. I never told anyone that I kneeled to pray, but trusted God to protect my back as I bowed in reverence before Him.

Those months of inactivity were wonderful for my spiritual life. I came to know a closeness with my God that I cherish. God had forced me, in a manner of speaking, to spend time alone with Him. I never blamed God for my accident, though from the beginning I realized that His sovereign hand was in my injury. As I studied God's Word, two subjects began to resolve themselves in my mind.

One was my abortion. I finally found the courage to confide my innermost feelings to my closest friend. Sherry faithfully visited me each week. She discipled me in a loving and caring way and she confided in me problems with which she was struggling. People have always confided in me, but somehow I had rarely trusted anyone to keep *my* secrets.

Finally, one day I could bear it no longer and said, "Sherry, I have something to tell you that I'm afraid might end our friendship."

"Nothing could do that, Pam."

"This might, but I've got to talk to somebody, and if you promise not to tell another soul, I'd like to talk to you."

"OK, what's troubling you so much that you're afraid to tell anyone?"

As I began to voice my deepest feelings regarding my abortion, the weight began to lift just a little. Sherry listened and did not condemn me. She told me God could get me through any problem and she promised to pray for me. Her encouragement and love helped strengthen me.

Sherry and I also discussed my growing desire to refrain from practices such as listening to popular music, watching TV shows and movies that contained blasphemies and sex, and other similar activities that other Christian friends participated in with clear consciences. I just didn't feel comfortable doing those things any longer.

For instance, one day Leigh and I decided to clean out our record collection. Hundreds of dollars worth of albums were destroyed that day as we joyfully discarded those we knew did not honor God by their lyrics or melodies. Afterward, a peace filled our home that was tangible in its reality.

Most of our friends thought we were crazy, but Sherry understood. One day she gave me the following and asked me to read it.

> If God has called you to be really like Jesus, He will draw you into a life of crucifixion and humility, and put upon you such demands of obedience, that you will not be able to follow other people, or measure yourself by other Christians, and in many ways He will seem to let other good people do things which He will not let you do. . . .
>
> The Lord may let others be honored and put forward, and keep you hidden in obscurity, because He wants you to produce some choice, fragrant fruit for His coming glory, which can only be produced in the shade. He may let others be great, but keep you small. He may let others do a work for Him and get the credit for it, but He will make you work and toil on without knowing how much you are doing; and then to make your work still more precious He may let others get the credit for the work which you have done, and thus make your reward ten times greater when Jesus comes.
>
> The Holy Spirit will put a strict watch over you, with a jealous love, and will rebuke you for little words and feelings, or for wasting your time, which other Christians never seem distressed over. So make up your

mind that God is an infinite Sovereign, and has a right to do as He pleases with His own. . . .

Settle it forever, then, that you are to deal directly with the Holy Spirit, and that He is to have the privilege of tying your tongue, or chaining your hand, or closing your eyes, in ways that He does not seem to use with others. Now when you are so possessed with the living God that you are, in your secret heart, pleased and delighted over this peculiar, personal, private, jealous guardianship and management of the Holy Spirit in your life, you will have found the vestibule of Heaven.

G.D. WATSON

That's how I want to live my life, Lord! Now I understand it's OK to be different from other people as long as what I do and say is done in accordance with Your Word. And thank You for Sherry, for a friend who understands.

Another frequent visitor was my former assistant manager. Cindy is one of the sweetest women I know; she deeply loves people, especially children. She had given up her job to become a full-time mother and I could see that raising little James brought her all the fulfillment a woman could need. We talked about things of the Lord. Cindy came to know Christ as her personal Saviour and I was privileged to see her begin to grow in love and knowledge of the Lord.

During my final few months at the store prior to my injury, I had begun to mellow a little toward my staff and customers. My new patience and caring attitude must have manifested itself at least once, because one day Cindy had come with a message for me. At the time she was still working at the store.

"Pam, do you remember that nasty woman who used to give you such a hard time? You know, the one you never could please, no matter what you did for her?"

"Not the one who wanted to match colors and nearly snapped my head off when I stopped her from cutting pieces off all the yarn skeins?" Every manager has one or two of these "jewels" who spend good money, but expect privileges beyond what can ethically be provided.

"That's her! Well, she came into the store yesterday asking for you. I didn't think you'd want me to give her your home phone number, so I took a message."

"What did she want this time?"

"She wanted to apologize for her behavior toward you. She said you had always been so patient with her. She said she has become a Christian and came to ask your forgiveness for her rude behavior toward you."

Tears welled up in my eyes. She wanted me to forgive her! I, who had served so many people with outward politeness and inward malice. She wanted my forgiveness!

Thank You again, Father! How good You are to show us by example how we should live our lives. And thank You for saving this woman whom I didn't care enough about to tell about You. I'm so grateful somebody loved her enough to tell her of Christ's love.

Trusting God

The second result my studies and the influence of godly people in my life had was to break down my stubborn will regarding having children. After consistently studying the Bible, I decided to yield myself completely to God. This included a willingness to become pregnant. This was doubly trusting God, because in addition to my mental fears, my physician advised against having children due to my physical condition. Now that I had a perfectly acceptable reason to avoid childbearing, I couldn't endure the thought of *not* getting pregnant!

Though both sex and pregnancy were "no-no's" because of my injury, Leigh and I began to live a normal sex life for the first time in six years of marriage. The freedom of having sexual relations without any qualms regarding the possibility of conception occurring is a delight known only to those who fully submit to God's will for marriage.

Only one dark spot remained—after months of trying, I had been unable to conceive. Because I had been on the pill for several years, my doctor advised that it might be over a year before I could conceive because of the effects of the lengthy use of the pill on my reproductive system. I was heartbroken.

Then one day, believing myself to be pregnant, I had a pregnancy test done. I was so sure, but the test came back negative. Dr. Eugene told me there was a simple procedure available to help me conceive. He suggested I make an appointment to have it done. I hesitated, asking if it would abort the baby should I be pregnant. Dr. Eugene assured me I wasn't pregnant, so that shouldn't be a concern of mine.

That same week, after nine months of virtual inactivity, my doctor informed me I could return to work on a limited basis. Joyfully, I called my store and talked to the assistant manager.

"Judy! I'm coming back to work next week. I wanted to let you know before they go and hire a new manager!" I said, laughing.

"Pam, you'd better call the district manager," Judy said. "She has to give you the OK, you know." Something was wrong; I could feel it in the pit of my stomach.

My employers had been super during my illness. They had held my job open for me, anticipating my return. Now, as I talked with my boss I learned that since my absence from work had continued for so long a period of time, in the best interests of the store a permanent new manager had been appointed to replace me—Judy. That was why she had been so reticent to say anything over the phone. She had been appointed only a few days earlier. I was assured of a desk job in the home office in another state. But I didn't *want* a desk job.

Why, God? I can't get pregnant and now I've lost the best job I ever had! Why? What are You trying to do to me?

Accepting God's forgiveness
Three weeks later I insisted the pregnancy test be redone. I was six weeks pregnant! I had been pregnant when it was determined I could return to work. God knew all about it and He also knew me! Just as He had had to wrench me from my job in the first place, so now He knew that had my job been waiting for me, I would have resumed my career, putting my priority as mother-to-be and full-time homemaker in second place again. God wanted me at home and that's where He had me.

Incidentally, my compensation payments stopped and our income was reduced to one-half of its original amount. Still we continued to give joyfully and regularly.

Trusting God in one area and seeing His faithfulness had encouraged me to trust Him in other areas, such as not permitting Dr. Eugene to do that procedure on me when that still small voice had said "wait."

When confronted with the fact I had been pregnant and the baby would have been aborted, Dr. Eugene nonchalantly treated the incident as of no importance. He performed abortions and knew I had had one. His opinion was that if I had lost this baby, it wouldn't have mattered. I could always have another. I asked not to be seen again by this doctor, one of four in a group, because I now understood that a physician who performs abortions has a different mindset regarding life and the sanctity of it.

My pregnancy was a bittersweet time of joy mingled with apprehension. I had absolutely no pain in my back, for carrying the baby held it in the correct position! However, though I had no physical pain, mentally I was far from healed.

Passing the twenty-third week was traumatic, as I vividly recalled my first baby and his horrendous death. But the worst times came when people would innocently ask, "Is this your first baby?"

Every inquiry as to the status of our family size forced me to remember this was not my first pregnancy, nor my first baby, nor even my first birth experience. Kind women assured me that delivery and labor were not as terrible as some would have me believe. Little did they know that I had already undergone a labor and delivery far in excess of most vaginal deliveries with respect to pain, both physical and mental.

Deception was the hardest part of being pregnant. I knew it was wrong to lie and finally settled on the phrase, "This is *our* first baby."

Why can't I just come out and tell them? Why do I have to have this terrible secret? Deception is wrong, I know it is! Hey world, this is not my first pregnancy! I know all about labor and the pain! I know! I know!

My physicians were not deceived. I was absolutely honest with them because I wanted the best medical care possible. Thirty-one years old when I became pregnant and at high risk because of the previous abortion, I knew my physicians could best treat me if they knew all the facts. Telling them was difficult, even knowing the confidentiality that exists between a woman and her doctor, because one of my doctors was also a member of our church. Every person who had to know about my abortion was a reminder that I had something to hide.

I tried concentrating on the fact that this baby was Leigh's and mine. He would be completely different than my first. *Anyway*, I reasoned, *that baby was part of my past. This baby brings to Leigh and me a bright, happy future.*

But I just couldn't keep my mind off the fact that this was my *second* baby, that I had killed my first child. *Will I never be able to forget, even for a moment? It's done. Over. God says He has forgiven me. Why can't I forgive myself?*

As the months rolled by, abortion came up several times in conversation. Always I remained silent, unable to participate in the discussion, wondering what these good Christian women would think of me if they knew I was one of those "cruel monsters" who had aborted her own child. *What right do I have to be pregnant after what I've done? How can God dare to trust me with a baby?*

Guilt still remained—not for the act itself, but for horror over the fact I could ever have done such a thing. Perhaps shame was more what I felt than guilt. That was it—I was so ashamed that my life had this terrible sin in its past, and so afraid those who knew my secret would one day inadvertently reveal it publicly.

During my pregnancy I opened up to Leigh about my abortion, pouring out my heart to him—crying, searching, worrying, still not quite believing that God would forgive and forget. I was deathly afraid that our baby would be born deformed or retarded as a sort of retribution for aborting my first child. I pleaded with God.

Finally, I began to pray for a happy, healthy baby if that would be God's will. On October 24, 1979, God gave us the desire of our hearts. Michael was born perfect in every way. At that moment, I finally accepted God's forgiveness for my abortion. To me, Michael was a visible declaration of God's grace and love. Unfortunately, I still had not learned to forgive myself.

Several months following Michael's birth, I was taking my turn at nursery duty at church one Sunday morning when a woman walked in with the tiniest baby I'd ever seen.

"Oh, how old is your baby?" I asked.

"Six months," she replied.

"But he's so tiny!"

"He was born prematurely when I was only six months pregnant," she smiled. "That's why he looks like a newborn when he's actually six months old."

My calm expression belied the emotions that welled up within me. *Dear God! Help me to cope with this! My son was only a few weeks younger than this when I aborted him! He might have been able to live like this one had he been born rather than aborted!*

Regardless of my desire to forget my past, I began to acknowledge the fact that my past would follow me wherever I went, to crop up when least expected or wanted.

THREE

Free at Last

Many incidents over the next four years of my life worked together as I entered the final stages of dealing with my abortion. It's not easy to separate them nor to define exactly the specific role each incident played, but I know that all things worked together for good, just as God promised.

Shortly before Michael's birth, Leigh and I had dedicated our lives to serving the Lord full-time wherever and whenever He chose. Since Leigh was prepared as a teacher, we planned to go to school so he could study the Bible in greater depth, later returning to our home church to teach in their Christian day school.

Within two years God had graciously given us the means to pay off all of our bills and in July 1981 we set off for seminary debt-free. Contented with our new home and life, I began to make friends easily for the first time in my life. Though it was difficult for me, I took the initiative in seeking other wives. Friendships grew as we discussed mutual interests of husbands in school and children at home. The fellowship was sweet and that first year at school is filled with precious memories.

That year I read a lot on abortion. I recall the first time I opened a magazine to an ad which showed a well-developed fetus, captioned by the words, "Abortion is more than a matter between a woman and her doctor." Revulsion gripped me in its icy fingers as I stared at that perfectly formed little body—and my baby had been older than that!

Since seminarians and their wives are naturally interested in issues of morality and ethics, the topic of abortion came up several times in discussions. Someone once asked, "What do you think it would be like to live the rest of your life having had an abortion?"

I silently listened as others conjectured, but an idea began to tickle my mind.

Shortly following my abortion I had recorded all the details of my experience, intending to write a book lauding the value of abortion as a means of escape for a woman caught between a rock and a hard place. I never wrote that book, a fact for which I'm eternally grateful. However, I kept all my notes and now I dug them out and refreshed my memory as to the actual details regarding my abortion. One morning I awoke before dawn and wrote out my story.

Writing out all the grizzly details helped in my healing process. It put things in their proper perspective as I was forced to see God's working in my life since my abortion, as well as evidences of His forgiveness for that sin.

My story was published in 1982 in a leading Christian magazine. *Anonymous* was used for my byline because Leigh and I weren't sure we wanted to tell the world about my sordid past and also because we wanted to spare his parents the embarrassment of having someone show them the magazine with the question: "Isn't this your daughter-in-law?" That article has since been published internationally and I'm still receiving comments as to its helpfulness. (Someone, who did not know I authored it, even suggested I read the article as part of the research for this book!)

A few months prior to writing the article on abortion, I had led a neighbor to the Lord. A new Christian, she placed me on a pedestal I neither wanted nor deserved. Connie had gotten pregnant and then had married the father of her child. She seemed well-adjusted, but felt guilty over being pregnant prior to marriage. One day Connie said, "You're so good—what's it like not to have any great sin in your life?"

Seeking a way to show her God forgives any and every sin, I gave her my article and asked her to read it. When she was done I said, "That's my story. I wrote that article. Now you know I'm not perfect either. I've shared this with you because I want you to know how right and brave you were to have your baby. Please don't tell anyone I'm the author of this article." *Another person keeping my secret! It's not right to ask people to keep my secret for me!*

When I sent the article to my old friend Sherry, she wrote back telling me how difficult it was for her to keep my secret from her husband. She was afraid she would "slip" and tell him one day. Suddenly I realized I'd come between a husband and wife by asking Sherry to tell no one. I'd never meant for that to happen and quickly wrote back that anything she knew about me I had automatically assumed she would feel free to confide to John. *My secret's affecting a lot of people who should never have been touched by my sin. When will it all end?*

Breaking a Sinful Habit

My emotional problems reached a peak after Leigh's first year at seminary. By August of 1982 I was both depressed and suicidal. But I valiantly kept my mask in place and few people knew about my secret inner turmoil. Finally, desperate to talk to someone, I called a woman friend and begged her to come over. She was not available, but within minutes her husband arrived to talk to me. I often wonder if I was Bob's first counseling case (he was a seminarian also), but his gentle yet honest advice put me on the road to recovery.

"Bob," I sobbed, "I want a divorce from Leigh. Our marriage was never meant to be and I can't go on this way much longer."

"Pam, why do you say your marriage was never meant to be? You guys have everything going for you!"

"Long ago I was told that when you go to bed with a man, you are married to that man in the sight of God, whether or not a ceremony is performed. I had sexual relations with a man prior to marrying Leigh. The other man is my husband in the sight of God, not Leigh. God can never honor this marriage because we married out of His perfect will. Suicide is the only way out for me now, I guess!"

Bob read me Scriptures proving the falsity of my beliefs. I had read them all before, and refused to acknowledge their truth.

"Besides, Tim and I conceived a child and I aborted that child to please him. How can God ever bless my marriage to Leigh? How can we go into ministry together with this murder in my past? Leigh deserves better than me!"

"First of all, Pam, do you really believe God would have you and Leigh divorce? What about Michael? Besides, Joan had an abortion and. . . . "

"What did you say?" I cut Bob off.

"Didn't you know about Joan's abortion? I guess I assumed she had told you!" Bob realized he had betrayed his wife's secret to me.

"Joan had an abortion? When? Has she managed to cope with it?"

I could hardly wait to see Joan, to finally talk with a woman who had been through an abortion and had resolved it completely.

After Bob left, Leigh and I sat down and discussed my bizarre insistence on our marriage not being condoned by God. It was not the first time Leigh had heard this from me. I knew it was a false insistence on my part, a way to avoid working out our problems, but I continued to maintain my position. My depression and suicidal tendencies, however, were very real and frightened Leigh more than me. Not knowing what else to do, he called our family physician in New York.

"Pam, what have you been eating?" Pete inquired after Leigh had described my symptoms.

"The usual—Coca-Cola and sweets. Can't seem to stay away from the chocolate, but it gives me energy when I'm tired, which is most of the time."

"Your eating habits are sin," replied Pete sternly. I felt conviction creeping in at the words of this good friend who was a Christian first and a medical doctor second. But Pete's cold confrontation irked me.

Boiling mad, I demanded, "Who are you to tell me my eating habits are sin? I've eaten like this all my life!"

"Unless you admit it's sin, Pam, the depression and mood swings will worsen. Your life will never get straightened out."

Pete talked with Leigh. As he hung up the phone, Leigh turned to me and gently informed me he was removing all Coke, caffeine products, and sugar from the house at once. I was in no state to argue, but lay limply on the bed and pitied my plight. In tears I told God my eating was sin and had been for many years. Dutifully concerned about the health of my husband and son, I had neglected my own health, eating junk foods and sweets instead of the nutritious well-balanced meals I provided for them. *All right, God, my eating habits are sin! Please remove all desire for Coke and sugar from my life. Only You can do it!*

For three nightmarish days Leigh and I endured my withdrawal symptoms together—me screaming with headaches and the shakes so bad I can hardly bear to recall them, and Leigh staying home from classes to nurse me through the ordeal. He never left my side and arranged for a close friend to care for Michael. *How can this man love me so much? Forgive me for doubting my marriage was ordained by You, Lord!*

For six months sugar and caffeine were removed from my life. No honey, no molasses, juice only if watered down so as to be almost tasteless, and no Coke or chocolate. Coke had been my worst addiction—I drank it morning, noon, and night by the gallon. Now we stayed home from socials where all those delicious goodies might be served. Leigh monitored me constantly. I couldn't even have white bread because it contained small amounts of sugar. But I began to recover.

To be honest, I felt better than I'd ever felt in my life and I came to a realization that greatly helped in resolving my abortion. Much of the distress I was encountering, which I blamed solely on my abortion, was due to problems, both mental and physical, that had become part of my life long before I ever aborted. Insecurity, irrational anger, and guilt over any and everything all accentuated my abortion experience, but had not caused the majority of the emotional turmoil. At the same time I realized that it didn't matter *what* had happened in my past; none of it justified my sinful responses to negative emotions. I knew that "if any man is in Christ, he is a new creature; the old things passed away; behold, new things have come" (2 Cor. 5:17).

Leigh and I counseled with a local pastor whom Bob had recommended. That dear servant of God made clear to me something that ended the confusion over my hatred of children and ill treatment of other people.

After in-depth questioning, Rev. Cane said, "Pam, there are basically two types of people—task oriented and people oriented. Neither is right nor wrong, but there has to be a balance. Leigh is people oriented and seems to have achieved a good balance. You, on the other hand, are task oriented to such an extreme that people are of little importance to you." He went on to discuss reaching that balance and learning to serve people rather than just shuffle papers.

Rev. Cane's wisdom revealed that much of my trouble with people came from my bent toward tasks. That knowledge, coupled with physical well-being due to a balanced diet, helped me to conquer my abortion problems as well as many others that had plagued me without my knowing it for most of my life.

Finding the Balance

After talking with Rev. Cane, I reflected over the weeks before we left home for seminary. Scared to death of becoming a pastor's wife, I had sought counsel from Pastor Langley.

"Someday," I began, "I'm going to be the wife of a pastor. But I'm not gentle or meek like your wife or any of the pastors' wives I know."

Pastor Langley replied with a twinkle in his eye, "Pam, gentleness and meekness are fruit of the Holy Spirit, and should be exhibited by all women and men. I thought you knew that."

I smiled. "You're right. I never thought of it that way."

Now, once again, I thought about the fruit of the Spirit which is "Love, joy, peace, patience, kindness, goodness, faithfulness, gentleness, self-control" (Gal. 5:22–23). I'd studied them off and on over the years, always trying to discern which I had and which I needed to obtain. Then it dawned on me that they aren't "obtained," but can only be manifested in a life devoid of anger, bitterness, frustration, guilt, and worry. They are produced by the Holy Spirit in a believer as he puts off practicing the sinful deeds of "immorality, impurity, sensuality, idolatry, sorcery, enmities, strife, jealousy, outbursts of anger, disputes, dissensions, factions, envying, drunkenness, carousing, and things like these" (vv. 19–21). The fruit of the Spirit exhibits itself each time a believer conquers these areas in any circumstance in his or her life. And it grows in each area as we continually practice God's Word with respect to the particular problem we are having.

Conviction stirred within me as I read over the list of sinful reactions to circumstances. *Which of these are still active in my life,* I wondered.

I concentrated on developing love because that was the fruit that was obviously least visible in my life. I studied 1 Corinthians 13 and 1 John. Love is so simple to receive yet so difficult to give—that is, to give as Christ gave it—unselfishly, sincerely, and without hesitation. But can I learn to love like that? I didn't *want* to love some of the people in my life.

Incidents sprang to my mind. Terrible bits from my early life that had turned me sour with bitterness and hate. I churned them over again and again in my mind whenever I felt like pitying myself or justifying my behavior.

I recalled my third-grade teacher, so unfeeling toward a small, shy little girl as she sang her heart out with the rest of the class preparing for a songfest which involved the entire school system.

"Someone is singing out of tune. Who is it?" she asked the class.

The songs were in unison and, unknown to me, my alto voice couldn't reach the pitch. "It's Pam," offered Scott.

"We can't have anything but beautiful music next week for all our parents and friends, can we? So Pam, please just move your lips to the words, but don't sing out loud."

I moved my lips to the words without singing out loud for nearly thirty years. Her scathing words had seared an almost permanent fear into my mind of being pointed out for something done incorrectly.

Another incident in my early adolescence triggered painful memories. I was in the seventh grade and it was time for the annual girl-ask-boy dance. There was a boy I liked who lived three doors down from me. I wanted to go to that dance and was determined to ask him. How I ever got the words out, I don't know, but Guy said he wasn't going. Later that day Guy came over to say he would go with me. Ecstatically, I picked out a peach-colored dress that I loved, but which did nothing to enhance my complexion. Mom fixed my hair up, but it really did look awful, no matter what she said to assure me. Guy arrived with a corsage—the first I'd ever received.

My parents drove us to the dance and then the nightmare began. Guy retreated into the boys' room and never came out. I sent someone in to find out what was wrong, thinking he might be ill, but Guy shouted through the door, "You don't think I'm going to be seen with you, do you? I only came because my mother made me come!" Mortified, I spent the entire evening alone as couples danced around me, carefully practicing the ballroom steps they had diligently learned in dancing class. For years I kept the picture taken that night—it showed the sad eyes and determined chin of a young girl standing alone under an arbor of roses.

We all have such events as these in our lives. Terrible moments of pain and hurt. Some of us cope better with them than others. I permitted my bad memories to steal my joy of living and to rob me of my self-esteem. Ashamed and fearful of rejection, I isolated myself from my family and limited my friendships only to the outcasts—the ones I knew couldn't hurt me. And I hated them because I knew I was one of them—laughed at, rejected, and ignored.

By the time Tim entered my life, I had come full circle and was an extroverted, loud, brassy young woman, still rejected and ignored, but able to hide my yearning for acceptance behind a false veneer of obnoxious behavior and scathing comments to any and all who dared to cross me. A desperate need to trust, combined with a deep longing to share the love I'd kept locked up inside of me, led me to open my heart to Tim, who represented acceptance to me.

Absorbed with my own need to be accepted by men, I never saw that God accepted me just the way He had made me. He had given me my personality and looks and gave me the opportunity to accept myself as He accepted me. Standing on God's power, I could have overcome those early incidents. But I stood alone, defiant of the people who cruelly ridiculed me. Expecting everyone I met to "put me down," I stored up bitter memories. When needed, I pulled one from my mind and thought about how I had been ruined by others.

Because I saw people as cruel and uncaring, I reciprocated in like manner. Yet what people thought of me was of vital importance. To be accepted, esteemed, and loved was my primary concern.

Hide your faults, Pam! Let no one see! Be strong; be forceful! Do a great job so that people notice you and have to accept you. Make yourself indispensable. I believed that people would accept me not for who I was, but for what I could do.

I finally permitted myself to see myself as God sees me. The Bible is the only mirror we can look into that gives us a true reflection of ourselves. God's Word forced me to see myself from the inside out, for God knows the heart as no human can.

After I admitted that I was bitter, angry, insecure, and intolerant of others, I began to study God's solutions to these sins in my life. "Let all bitterness and wrath and anger and clamor and slander be put away from you, along with all malice. And be kind to one another, tender-hearted, forgiving each other, just as God in Christ also has forgiven you" (Eph. 4:31–32).

I made a list of all those against whom I harbored bitter thoughts: my third-grade teacher, Guy, and a host of others who had hurt me over the years. I included Tim, for I'd finally come to realize that I hated him more than words could tell. Then there were those who had encouraged me to abort or who had not hindered my "flight to freedom." I asked God's forgiveness for my sinful attitude toward these and then I forgave them in my heart before God. I mean I *really* forgave them.

Finally, I made right with all those whom I had knowingly hurt. My list was long and saying, "I'm sorry, will you forgive me?" wanted to stick in my throat each time. Hardest was seeking Leigh's forgiveness. I went to him and asked his forgiveness for being an ungodly wife and for the angry words I had spoken. When my task was done, a deep inner peace and joy, and yes, even love, that God wants to exhibit in each believer, had replaced the guilt and shame as the walls I'd built one-by-one to shield myself from pain came crumbling down.

In all my searching, one truth had never reached my mind until now—God's forgiveness is a wonderful thing. It frees us from the bondage of sin. But we can only enjoy that forgiveness as we forgive others just as God has so freely forgiven us. And that ultimate forgiveness can come only after all has been made right, for only then can we forgive ourselves. I have forgiven myself for believing that I was inferior simply because others said I was, and I've forgiven myself for failing to trust God to see me through all the difficult circumstances in my life, including my untimely pregnancy.

I'm still a "task person." A lifetime of conditioning doesn't disappear overnight, at least it didn't for me. I still make some bad mistakes in dealing with people, but I've learned to make amends right away. And when people say things that hurt (which doesn't happen as often as I imagined it would), I forgive them in my heart, knowing that I too have caused pain to others because of unthinking comments. I'm really beginning to love people and to see them as not inherent in the task, but as the reason for the task. I'm still learning to love the sinner and to hate his sin, but where I once stumbled and fell, I now walk with confidence.

A Skeleton in Every Closet
Talking with Joan about our abortions really helped to settle things in my mind. Shyly I approached her. "Did Bob tell you he's spilled the beans about your abortion and that I had one too? Do you mind talking about it?"

Joan's experience was different from mine. She had been only eight weeks pregnant, had aborted more recently than I, had not really loved the father, and had completely resolved it in her mind. "I have to tell myself that God has completely forgiven me and it's sin to fail to forgive myself," she said.

"Do other people know?"

"No. In fact, Bob was a little upset he had let it slip to you. Very few people know and no one here at school even suspects. We just never mention it anymore."

"Why don't you tell anyone?"

"Because it's in the past and there's no reason to bring it up."

"I think other women can be helped by what we have been through." I gave her a copy of my article to read.

Around we went, Joan arguing for silence and me wanting to find the courage to tell others that abortion was not the answer. Talking with Joan, sharing our mutual thoughts regarding our actions, and confiding to each other details of our abortions helped me tremendously. Was Joan right? Was it best forgotten? Dwelling on the abortion and permitting oneself to feel guilty was sin. But I knew there were other women who were hurting just as I had hurt.

Leigh and I considered how and if to make a public statement. We had already informed pastors we knew that, should the need arise, I was available to counsel women who had aborted or who were considering an abortion. But my concern was for the women who were suffering and might never openly admit to anyone, even their pastor or closest friend, that they had once aborted. These women deserved help too.

Leigh worked hard preparing for the pastorate. My fears haunted me. *What will people think of Leigh when they discover his wife is a murderer? Will anyone want him to minister to them? Will I be accepted? How will I face fellow Christians and look them in the eye?* You see, I was still guilty of the sins of worry and fear.

Once again I sought the counsel of a wise and godly man. He said those who would hold it against me for having had an abortion would only find something else to hold against me if I had not had the abortion. Some people will never realize that past sin that has been confessed, repented of, and forgiven is just that—past. So I decided to adopt the philosophy, "In God have I put my trust; I will not be afraid of what man can do to me" (Ps. 56:11, KJV).

As opportunities arose, I began to let people know about my abortion. Do you know what I discovered? People who had never spoken to me approached me. They did not condemn me, but encouraged me to write this book and told me of people they knew who had aborted and needed to come to terms with their act. God is so good! Had I kept it to myself, His love would never have been displayed through the people I once feared. I saw my fear of others knowing my secret was merely a reflection of my old fear of rejection.

There are events in each of our lives which we are not proud to admit we took part in, but if telling someone about our past and God's working in us can help that other person come to grips with their problem, then I believe God is honored. It would be pure selfishness on my part to keep silent because of fear when another person could be assisted by hearing what I learned through my experience.

It's still hard sometimes to openly admit I aborted. The words sort of catch in my throat each time I say, "I had an abortion." But oh, it's helped me to say them aloud. And yes, there have been rough moments as I've shared my experience with others. Reactions range anywhere from shock, to rebuke, to silent disbelief, to pity. I guess part of the reason is that I've been a Christian for a long time and people forget that we all have some kind of a skeleton in our closets. Want to know something? As a reminder to me that no one is exempt from having a secret sin in their past, I have a six-foot cardboard skeleton hanging on the inside of the door of our guest closet. When people see it they always remark, "What's that?" And I reply, "Oh, I thought *everyone* had a skeleton in their closet."

Since telling people that I aborted, God has shown me in tangible ways His care for me. My healing process has only been completed since I have conquered my fear and worry by trusting God in a practical way. Secrecy leads to fear and worry that others may find out. I cannot tell you the relief I have now that others know. You see, now I have nothing to hide!

Today, when I speak on the topic of abortion, I do so with tears in my eyes. Abortion will always be an emotional topic for me, but now I cry for others because I know that to any group I may address, I can look out over the audience and say, "I know some of you hearing my words have had an abortion and are hurting deep inside. But I want you to know that there is hope, that by God's grace you can go from victim to victor."

Make no mistake, the road back has been long and hard. It takes time to erase the years of hatred, bitterness, and self-pity. I had to learn to live with the fact that an abortion, once accomplished, can never be reversed. I made my choice and I paid the price, but Someone else bears my burden now. Today I am free.

UNDERSTANDING ABORTION

F O U R

Abortion American Style

Since the 1973 Supreme Court decision legalizing abortion, over 18 million babies have died by their mothers' consent. Induced abortion was the most common elective surgical procedure in America in 1982. That year there were 54,652,000 women in the United States between the ages of 15 and 44; with over 13 million known abortions in the years 1972–1982, 24 percent or one in four women of childbearing age have aborted. In 1982 almost one third of all known pregnancies were aborted.[1]

Why? What makes a woman deny all reason and rush to abort her unborn child?

Perhaps you've never considered what the abortion law actually says. I hadn't until recently. What I discovered shocked me to the core of my being.

On January 22, 1973, the Supreme Court of the United States ruled in a 7 to 2 majority decision in *Roe vs. Wade* to permit abortion under the following guidelines: In the first trimester the decision to abort lies solely with the woman and her doctor; in the second trimester, though a state cannot stop an abortion, it can regulate abortion procedures which may be hazardous to the woman's health; in the third trimester, a state may forbid abortion except in the instance where the abortion is needed to preserve a woman's life or health.

During the first trimester (first 3 months) of a pregnancy every woman experiences some depression, some "bad" feelings, due to the hormonal changes taking place in her body. A person who is depressed is apt to make decisions based on her feelings rather than on facts. Everything looks so gloomy when one is "down in

58

the dumps." The thought of carrying a baby for nine months, and then the ensuing responsibilities of caring for a child, can seem insurmountable, even with a planned pregnancy. We just don't see things in their proper perspective when we are depressed. Dr. John Willke states:

> What is absolutely crucial to understand, however, is that how a woman feels in the first three months of her pregnancy and how she will feel in the last three months of her pregnancy, are commonly totally different. If all upset women with unwanted pregnancies had been aborted in years past, at least one third of our readers would not be living today.[2]

The first trimester is the time when most abortions are performed, so we see that most women decide to abort during a time in their lives when life-changing decisions should not be made.

According to the law, the woman and her doctor are to make the abortion decision. Frequently, however, women do not consult their personal doctors when they anticipate abortion. The physician, usually a gynecologist/obstetrician, has an obligation to care for the woman *and* her unborn child, but often obligingly confirms that the baby should be aborted. Pro-abortion physicians seem to "forget" that they have *two* patients who deserve *equal* concern and care.

During the second trimester, certain abortion procedures can be refused due to the risks involved to the woman. Still, the woman's legal right to abort is in no way jeopardized; it is in the method to be used that her choice is restricted.

In the third trimester a woman may abort if her life or health is in peril. Dr. C. Everett Koop, U.S. Surgeon General, says that "abortion as a necessity to save the life of the mother is so rare as to be almost nonexistent."[3] Dr. Landrum Shettles in *Rites of Life* states: "In more than forty years of obstetrical and gynecological practice, I have seen only a 'handful' of cases where abortion was needed to save a woman's life."[4]

It is a fact that many abortions are performed in the third trimester, and since physical life is not being preserved for the woman, we can assume it is her "health" which necessitates the abortion. If not referring to her physical life, then "health" must refer to the woman's mental attitude—stress caused by emotional, physical, economic, or social reasons. If we women are honest with each other, we will admit that any pregnancy brings stress in one or more of these areas depending upon the circumstances surrounding a particular pregnancy. And who is to know how great our stress really is? A woman can be very convincing to herself and to others if she is desperate enough to rid herself of an untimely pregnancy. She may go so far as to threaten or even attempt suicide in an effort to get her own way.

Essentially, then, the ruling of the Supreme Court can be summed up in one sentence: Women of the United States may abort their unborn babies for any or no reason at any time throughout their nine months of pregnancy. Dr. Koop states, "In the whole spectrum of abortion laws, the most liberal policies exist in the U.S. where the unborn child has no legal protection up until the moment of birth."[5] To this might be added—in many states the baby aborted alive has no protection because his live "birth" was not intended!

Freedom and Rights

Women of America were given the legal right to abortion-on-demand by the 1973 Supreme Court decision, but does that automatically mean we are morally free to choose to act on that right? The law, try as it may, cannot enforce morality. The truth of the matter is we have always had the freedom, the responsibility, and the privilege of choosing to carry our babies to term. The difference is that now millions of us are abusing our freedom as we rush to take advantage of our *right*.

Speaking of freedom, I recognize I have a choice of exercising or not exercising my right, both moral and legal. Take, for instance, my legal right to drive through an intersection when the green light is in my favor. However, though legally right, I do not have the moral freedom to exercise my right, if, as I begin to pass through the intersection, I see a car coming from my left, speeding through his red light. Though it is my legal right to go through the intersection, I am no longer morally free to do so and I now give up my legal right for the safety of myself and others.

So too it should be with abortion. Though a pregnant woman knows she can legally abort, she should consider whether she is indeed morally free to do so.

Confusion often arises when a woman listens to pro-abortionists. These people would have us believe that women need to have the right to choose whether to have a child at *any* given point in time. Look at what they say:

> Supporting safe, legal abortions do indeed respect life. So much in fact, that we believe medically supervised care should be available to women who conclude that an unwanted pregnancy must not continue. We are not "pro-abortion," a fact our critics are unable to grasp. We support the right of every individual to freedom of conscience in matters of reproductive choices and access to good quality medical care, including the provision of abortion services, for all women.[6]

Pro-abortionists want us to believe that they are pro-choice. However, the woman who consents to an abortion usually is not making an *informed* decision; she thinks she has no option but to abort. She is doing the only thing she knows to rid herself of her burden as she flees in a desperate escape to a dead-end of "do it" (abort) or "it" (the baby) will ruin your life.

Pro-abortionists refer to anti-abortionists as "anti-choice" because they conclude that abortion is the "right" choice, indeed the only choice in an untimely pregnancy. Pro-choice is equated with freedom of choice, but

> we hear a lot of talk about freedom of choice, but that involves an intelligent decision based upon two alternatives backed by information. What's going on in the abortion clinics is not freedom of choice. It's manipulation because of a woman's ignorance. Even women who are educated and intelligent don't know what they are doing.[7]

Perhaps we need to examine the word *choice. Webster's Dictionary* defines *choice* as "the act or power of choosing; a selecting or separating from two or more things that which is preferred; . . . carefully selected, worthy of being preferred; select; precious."[8] In other words, to make a choice we must carefully examine available options. Only then can we choose the thing worthy of being preferred.

I have been told time and again by women who have aborted

that they never really felt they *had* a choice; they were told that their unborn babies were merely blobs of tissue, and that the problems they would face if they allowed their pregnancies to continue to birth would be unresolvable. A responder to my questionnaire explains:

> I firmly believe that "pro-choice" would be better put as being "no choice." *How* can a young girl or woman make that type of choice while under severe emotional/mental/stress/anguish and also while experiencing physical hormonal changes?

Yet every woman who has aborted has chosen to do so. She must face that fact. So also every woman who bears her child to term does so because she did indeed make a choice. In fact, if a woman has chosen *not* to abort, it would be safe to assume that she has considered the facts and made an informed decision.

Faye Wattleton, President of Planned Parenthood, stated in 1980 that "Planned Parenthood has a tradition of informing its patients of the risks and benefits of services they request. There's a difference between 'informed' consent and emotional harassment."[9]

In response to that statement, I quote from a questionnaire completed by a woman who experienced Planned Parenthood's information: "For eight years I've been trying to get over my feelings of hatred and anger towards the people at Planned Parenthood who lied to me. They said, 'It's not a baby—it's just a blob like a wart.'"

Indeed, pro-choice groups do not *want* informed consent available to pregnant women, because in their opinion the laws are

> not designed to ensure that a woman receive the information necessary to make a knowledgeable decision about whether to terminate her pregnancy. Rather, they require that the physician provide the woman with a variety of questionable and disturbing information, such as a statement that the fetus is a human being from the moment of conception, a detailed description of the appearance and characteristics of the fetus, and a list of medical risks. . . . They also impose a waiting

period, usually of 24 or 48 hours, between the time the woman gives consent and the performance of the abortion. These requirements are clearly intended to discourage women from choosing abortion and to burden that choice.[10]

People who want women to abort do not want basic information to reach pregnant women. The pro-choice people have gotten their wish; the informed consent laws were struck down as unconstitutional. This is regrettable, for knowing the facts about abortion could make all the difference. As for information regarding the development of the child and medical risks to the woman causing emotional harassment: "The facts are convincing enough. You don't need emotion to sway opinion in this case."[11]

Though the facts speak for themselves, maybe what we do need is a little honest emotion, some sincere tear-shedding over the horror that is abortion. Emotions are a God-given means for responding to situations that bring joy or sorrow or trouble to us. Let's stop pretending we are cold, hard stones—we feel pain and react to it long before we are born. An honest release of emotions might clear the air by revealing what people truly believe deep inside. To suppress your emotions when faced with the facts of abortion is to wear a mask held in place by the rigid arms of self-deception.

People who want abortion-on-demand to abound have taught us well to deal on the surface, ignoring those deep inner convictions that prick our consciences to stop with horror and take a look at what we are about to do. Indeed, we have been so conditioned by pro-choice that even when we know what our actions will involve, we are able to continue coldly down the path of abortion. Sorrowfully our feelings too often are held in check until following the abortion, when they break forth, at times unrestricted over the choices we have made.

Dr. Jean Garton states, "A misapplication of the 'freedom to choose' can alter a society's perception of reality."[12] Gradually people begin to tolerate what they once would have abhorred—slavery, holocaust, abortion. Elisabeth Elliot pinpoints the fallacy in the entire pro-choice argument: "What proponents of abortion never say, is that the choice they defend is the choice to kill people."[13]

Because we have a legal right to abort does not mean the

choice to abort is the responsible alternative to carrying a baby to term. Abortion will prove to have been the wrong choice if we carefully and seriously ponder the entire matter.

"Help" for Women

Since 1795, laws have existed in every state to protect the unborn. These were all negated by the 1973 Supreme Court decision on abortion.

Because the arguments are intricately interwoven, sorting out the reasons liberal abortion was legalized is tantamount to working a 1,000 piece jigsaw puzzle with your eyes closed! But our eyes need to be wide open as we see that "helping" women is stressed to the exclusion of the unborn baby's wishes.

Presented here are eight popular arguments given by pro-abortionists as they pushed to overrule the unborn's right to protection under the law in order that we women could have a choice. These arguments continue to be advocated today.

1. *The safety of the woman.* Statistics were cited by the NARAL (National Association for the Repeal of Abortion Laws) indicating that 5,000 to 10,000 deaths per year occurred following illegal abortions. Dr. Bernard Nathanson in his book, *Aborting America*, now admits the figures were fraudulent, concocted to convince the Supreme Court of the need to legalize abortion.[14] The actual figures show a total of 90 deaths from *all* abortions in 1972, the year prior to national legalization of abortion.[15] Had we any common sense, we would have realized that

> it is most difficult today to hide a death from abortion. If the woman is brought to the hospital alive, she is usually suffering from hemorrhage or infection, both clear indications of the cause of her trouble. If the woman dies before getting to the hospital or immediately on arrival, the laws of most states require an autopsy which would quickly reveal the recent abortion. Unless the woman's body is hidden or destroyed, awkward and unlikely feats, it is virtually impossible to conceal the abortion death.[16]

Those concerned with the safety of the woman choosing to abort make little mention of a statute that was voided the same day as the Supreme Court decided on *Roe vs. Wade.* It was determined in *Doe vs. Bolton* that Georgia's abortion statute set unreasonable conditions for abortions in matters such as hospital accreditation (this meant clinics could open and operate freely) and confirmation by two independent physicians (this meant a woman could seek and find a doctor who would agree to abort her).

Those who were so concerned for the safety of the woman now cried over regulations geared to provide safe conditions for abortions:

> In some states, laws require that abortion clinics have blood supplies, knee- or foot-controlled sinks, wide hallways, and elevators, and that they pay licensing fees. These regulations, *which are unrelated to maternal health matters*, can make it prohibitively expensive to operate a clinic. Several of these ordinances have been struck down [italics added].[17]

How can a person concerned with the safety of the woman state that a requirement of blood supplies is unrelated to maternal health? Expensive, yes, but unrelated to the woman's safety in a surgical procedure? Hardly!

The arguments for legalizing abortion for the safety of the woman assumed *legal* abortions would automatically be *safe* abortions. Though most women don't die, the incidence of permanent and temporary physical injuries is high[18] and the extent of emotional aftermath women face will never be accurately assessed.

2. *Liberal abortion laws would cut down on illegal abortions.* Nobody knows how many abortions were performed illegally prior to lessening of the restrictions. Estimates vary depending on the source, but range from 200,000 to over 1 million per year prior to 1973.

Unfortunately, crime continues to flaunt the law. Because the Supreme Court forbade state regulations for early abortions, many clinics have cropped up to compete for the lucrative business. Some are "legal," but are hardly better than their illegal counterparts. In addition, illegal abortions

> may have become more dangerous after legalization. Since *physicians who were performing illegal abor-*

tions can now provide them in a controlled atmosphere, illegal abortions may now be performed primarily by untrained individuals or by women themselves [italics added].[19]

Illegal clinics could not operate were it not for the women who continue to utilize their services.

> The reason is human nature. When the law sanctions abortions, it is often regarded too casually: Many no longer question its safety or moral implications, and "back-street" abortions offer anonymity, lower cost, and a quick arrangement without records or red tape.[20]

3. *Women have always had abortions and will always continue to do so, so why not legalize them?* Ancient writings tell us that women aborted and many ancient cultures outlawed abortion to *diminish* its practice. Still, abortions were performed. Because something is illegal doesn't mean people won't choose to do it. There have always been and always will be people who are desperate enough to go above the law to obtain their desired end.

4. *It would be cheaper to abort than to support the baby.* This argument supports the premise that the state would bear the brunt, through welfare, of paying for the child were he to be born. This view selected the poor as targets for abortions simply because they cannot pay their own way. No one can argue the fact that it *is* more expensive to raise a child to adulthood than to spend $300 for an abortion. Those who hold to this view forget that in America we assist the poor financially without restriction as to how many children a given woman might bear. Our liberal abortion laws discriminate against and are unfair to poor women, relegating their lives and the lives of their unborn children to a matter of dollars and cents.

5. *Rigid abortion laws discriminate against the poor.* The "rich," it was argued, could afford to travel to a jurisdiction where legal abortions could be obtained, whereas the "poor" were forced to have children they neither wanted nor could care for since they could not afford legal abortions.

John Frame succinctly summarizes the problem with this argument:

The fallacious premise of this reasoning, however, is that if rich people are able to do something wrong, the law should make it easy for poor people to do it too.[21]

In this country we've adopted an attitude of "You owe it to me—it's my *right.*" This attitude displays selfish concern for "me" rather than sacrificial concern for others. Not everyone has the same advantages in life, nor the same talents, nor the same intellect. To claim that a particular thing is "owed to me" because I am poor or rich, white or black, man or woman, adult or child, is to place ourselves in a position that was not relegated to us.

We forget that "in God we trust" and all that we have comes to us by His grace, including our "life, liberty, and pursuit of happiness." Let's be certain we don't use our liberty to the detriment of others, for true happiness comes from putting someone else's rights ahead of ours.

6. *Legalized abortion is a means of population control.* We were told that there were millions of starving people in this over-crowded world. True—there are starving people, but many starve because of malnutrition (improper diet), not from lack of food. In countries such as India, many people refuse to eat available meat because of their religious beliefs. They also refuse to kill any form of animal life lest they should destroy a "reincarnated" being. In other countries famine causes a lack of food—when famine occurs, food is scarce.

Neither is the problem space. Vast land areas go wasted when they could be used to grow food or house people. Two-thirds of the earth's people live on less than 2 percent of the land.[22] In America we are indeed sparsely populated. "It [America] has a population of 56 persons per square mile, compared with England's 586, Japan's 708, and Holland's 982."[23] Americans comprise approximately 6 percent of the world's population, but we consume about 30 percent of the world's food supply.[24] In America no one needs to be denied the right to be born because of lack of food or space.

Since 1957 our population has steadily decreased. In 1972 the U.S. fertility rate dropped below replacement levels. Healthy adoptable babies have virtually been eliminated. Soon we may very well find ourselves with more people over sixty than under sixty. What abortion is achieving, in essence, is a disproportionate number of "older" people in relation to the number of younger people. Only the future will show what the nonexistence of millions of children will mean in terms of educators trained to teach children that aren't here, jobs with no one present to fill them, the imbalance of wage earners to those retired, causing diminished buying and selling power, and a social security system that becomes defunct because so much more went out than came in.

7. *Abortion is safer than childbirth.* Having had an abortion and subsequently three living children, I ask the question—safer for whom? Obviously, the aborted child dies. The woman will probably live, but may have emotional and physical trauma.

However, statisticians do not include ectopic pregnancies with abortions. An ectopic pregnancy occurs when the fertilized egg remains in the fallopian tube rather than descending to the uterus. As the embryo grows, the tube ruptures causing serious complications for the woman. An ectopic pregnancy must always be terminated. However, the procedure of removing the ectopic pregnancy is not classified as an abortion. If it were, there would be no question that childbirth is far safer than abortion. Dr. Willke comments:

> It is common today to read the statements of all sorts of uninformed people who say that delivery of a child is more dangerous to the mother than a legal abortion. This is simply not true. Abortion of any type, at any stage of pregnancy, is at least twice as likely to take her life as childbirth.[25]

Let's face facts: a woman's body was made to carry and bear children as a normal process. Abortion is an induced trauma forced upon the woman's body against its natural purpose.

8. *The woman's right to privacy.* An unmarried pregnant woman using the pseudonym "Miss Roe" to protect her identity, contended that in her home state of Texas there existed a law which was unconstitutional since it denied her the right to obtain an abortion because she did not need it to save her life.

This case was decided by the Supreme Court on January 22, 1973. Using the 9th and 14th Amendments to back up their decision, Justice Blackmun expressed the views of the seven concurring members of the Court. In part, the decision stated that laws permitting abortion only to save the life of the mother were unconstitutional because they interfered with the right of privacy, which the Court held to include a woman's decision of whether or not to terminate a pregnancy.[26]

Let us note here the comments from the two dissenting judges. Justice Byron White wrote:

> I find nothing in the language or history of the Constitution to support the Court's judgment. . . . The Court apparently values the convenience of the pregnant mother more than the continued existence and development of the life or potential life which she carries.

Justice William Rehnquist wrote, "I have difficulty in concluding, as the Court does, that the right of 'privacy' is involved in this case." When we hear the word *privacy,* we think of something most precious to us—freedom from interference in our lives from others; the right to live as we choose within the framework of the law. We believe privacy is guaranteed by our Constitution, and although it is inferred, the fact is that *privacy* is not mentioned in that document.

Does any person have the right to privacy when the act they intend to perform jeopardizes the life or well-being of another? No. As Claire Chambers states:

> Our blessing of liberty carries with it certain responsibilities which cannot be ignored. The liberty of an individual, therefore, must *of necessity* be limited. A man is free to act so long as he does not infringe upon the life or liberty of another. He may also take a risk or place his own life in jeopardy, so long as he does not endanger the life of another thereby. In other words, the State has no jurisdiction over *personal* morals, so long as only one person is involved; but beyond that it must intervene.[27]

When more than one person is involved, privacy becomes public.

All people are guaranteed the right *not* to be deprived of life, liberty, and property nor denied equal protection under the law according to the 14th Amendment.

We must remember that privacy is not isolation from interaction with other people. Claiming the right to privacy can become a cloak to avoid listening to and heeding advice we may not want to hear. People need each other in their privacy. Our rights should be based on the mutual rights of those with whom we coexist. Even so, the privacy of the pregnant woman has been so protected as to exclude even the father or the parents (of a minor) from having a say in the life and death decision regarding an unborn child.[28]

Each of us must consider when our personal right to privacy ends. For instance, I have the right to privacy in my own home. People cannot simply barge in and invade that privacy. However, if a person rushes through the front door of his neighbor's house to rescue a child whose mother is beating him unmercifully, that person has indeed invaded another person's privacy, but with cause to another's welfare. A right to privacy ends when a person places another's life in peril.

So with the woman who intends to abort. The invasion of her privacy should be for the purpose of insuring her welfare *and* that of her unborn child. Our right to privacy is limited by the need to enter each other's lives in order to help someone avoid causing harm to another person. We are responsible for what we do as well as for what we allow to be done to others—we are our brothers' keepers.

Melody Green, in her pamphlet "The Questions Most People Ask About Abortion," writes:

> Our laws are very funny. They allow police to enter the privacy of people's homes to stop them from battering and abusing their children, and then they use the same force of law to guarantee the "privacy and right" of parents to grind up their babies before birth.[29]

Our right to privacy must end when our intended action would cause harm to another as we strive to gain selfish satisfaction in a given area.

One comment regarding the Supreme Court's ruling on abortion: Though I do not agree with its decision, out of fairness to the Court, I surmise that in considering all of the arguments, they probably acted to some extent out of compassion for women who desperately wanted an abortion and were about to get one regardless of the consequences. What the Court and no one else anticipated was that women would swarm to clinics by the millions to abort. Obviously, the majority of women who had untimely pregnancies and were not desperate enough to go beyond the law, now decided to take advantage of their legal "right" to choose.

President Ronald Reagan puts it succinctly when he counters what has resulted by stating:

> Make no mistake, abortion-on-demand is not a right granted by the Constitution. No serious scholar, including one disposed to agree with the Court's result, has argued that the framers of the Constitution intended to create such a right.[30]

Purposefully Used

There are always underlying motives behind a person's reasons for fighting for any given cause. For instance, those who diligently campaign to keep drunken drivers off the roads do so for the *reasons* that drunken drivers cause accidents and maim or kill people. But the *motivation* behind a drunk driving campaign is often the fact that an advocate's life was personally affected by a drunk driver. Here the motivation is noble.

Consider now the people who pushed for liberal abortion laws. They campaigned for the woman's safety, the poor, population control, and the right to privacy. We have seen that these reasons, though posited as arguments concerned with helping women, can be easily refuted. The motives behind the reasons, however, need no refutation. They stand blatantly out in the open showing the greed and self-fulfillment that truly lie at the base of the pro-abortion movement. These motives are now presented and clarified so that you might know that the guise of concern for women is merely a deception. Indeed, the reasons for pushing for liberal abortion laws served as a flimsy camouflage for the personal motives that lie at the heart of the "right to choose" campaign.

Abortion is big business, doing an estimated one-half billion dollars worth of business each year. Let's face it, staff personnel at an abortion clinic are not about to adequately present a fair case for why a woman should *not* abort. They would be depleting their own coffers. Like forcing an evolutionist who teaches in a public school to present creationism alongside evolution, one view will always be presented with bias to the detriment of the other because a person will naturally advocate his own position more forcefully than the opposing view.

Did you know that scientists want and need humans for research? What better way to obtain human beings than through legal means? Dr. Willke's *Handbook on Abortion* includes a photograph of a doctor experimenting on a living, legally aborted human baby. The doctor explains, "We are simply using something which is destined for the incinerator to benefit mankind. . . . Of course, we would not dream of experimenting with a viable child."[31] Dr. Koop says:

> There is no doubt some researchers are experimenting upon live aborted babies. Bizarre as it may seem, vivisection is being practiced on human fetuses while the same procedure on animals is widely condemned.[32]

There is evidence that some cosmetic companies use human collagen (a gelatin-like substance found in bone and cartilage) from aborted babies in their products. "Unless your beauty product specifies animal collagen or bovine collagen, the product probably contains human collagen," since the "Food and Drug Administration does not require pretesting or the identification of cosmetic ingredients."[33]

Medicine also makes use of aborted pre-born children: "A rabies vaccine is produced from viruses grown in the lungs of aborted children, according to the FDA. A polio vaccine was also grown with cells from aborted kids."[34]

All this leads to a greater reason for the abortionist to actively recruit women to abort their unborn children. Think about it— the abortionist gets paid for performing the abortion ($150 to $1,000 for as little as 15 minutes' work). He then gets paid *again* when he sells the aborted babies for research.[35]

Some people believe they are doing something for the good of mankind by advocating abortion. They see abortion as one method of eliminating "undesirable" people (deformed, retarded, poor) in favor of creating a race of superior people.

The right of society to continue to exist and to become
increasingly free of genetic and environmental handi-
caps seems more important than the right of an individual to act against the welfare of children and society [by
bearing "inferior" children]. Man determines his future
whether he likes it or not. He should choose to determine it purposefully rather than blindly.[36]

Will we soon be killing off already-born people because they
don't match up to a prescribed norm? Indeed, we see seeds of this
beginning to germinate in such cases as Infant Doe, who was left
to die because of a birth defect. President Reagan states, "We
cannot survive as a free nation when some men decide that others are not fit to live and should be abandoned to abortion and
infanticide."[37]

But more importantly, we must ask *who* is the most qualified
to decide who should live and who should die? Physicians? Parents? Judges? Or should we leave the choice to God?

Some people wanted liberal abortion laws so they could use
abortion as a backup to failed contraceptive measures. Linda
Francke's statement sums up well the feeling on this view: "While
birth control has drastically shifted the odds in the prevention of
unwanted pregnancies, accidents will happen."[38]

An important forerunner of the abortion-on-demand law was
Griswold vs. Connecticut which was decided in 1965. This case
determined that the use of contraceptives within the marriage
relationship was a private matter between the husband and wife.

The decision can be read as establishing the right of a
married couple to decide if and when they wish to have
children. . . . The whole emphasis of the traditional
view of marriage handed down to us from our Judeo-
Christian origins was on the *procreation* of children,
not on limitation of their number.[39]

Today, it is a widespread practice for married people to "plan"
their families. If the planning fails, abortion is available as an ap-
proved and accepted means of removing the "obstacle" to a couple's preplanned life. For those determined not to have children,
abortion serves as a convenient backup to contraception—a fail-
safe, if you will. Twenty-one percent of the abortions performed

in 1982 were on married women in order to remove "accidents."

Pro-abortionists admit that "abortion is inferior . . . to pregnancy prevention as a mode of birth control" but still insist that it "should be available as a second-line method of family planning."[40] Dr. Kenneth Edelin's thinking typifies this view:

> [Abortion] is not the ideal method of birth control and should not be used as such. . . . When birth control fails, a woman has a right to have her pregnancy terminated in a safe and professional manner.[41]

Steve Waterhouse states that a person must be ignorant of the facts or inconsistent to consider abortion as a legitimate means of birth control.[42] Susan Foh states:

> A more important and basic aspect of the solution [to untimely pregnancies] is a change in attitudes and values, a return to "traditional" morality—biblical morality. Sexual intercourse must be put back into its proper context, marriage. In addition, persons need to be reeducated to accept responsibility for their own action, that is, to acknowledge that sexual intercourse, even with contraception, may result in pregnancy; therefore, if one engages in sex, he or she must be willing to accept the responsibility for a child . . . children are a gift from God. The unplanned conception is not a curse but a blessing.[43]

But unplanned pregnancies among married women were not the major motive for liberalizing abortion laws. In 1982, 79 percent of the abortions in the United States were done on unmarried women.[44] Today, abortion serves primarily as a backup to or in place of contraception to eliminate "accidents" caused by unmarried couples. Abortion in these instances treats only the symptom, for the disease is sexual promiscuity.

Speaking from personal experience, I find it an abomination that abortion serves as an alternative to abstinence prior to and outside of marriage. When two people consent to sexual intercourse, they should be fully aware that their act might produce a situation wherein one plus one equals three. Foh sums it up well:

But sexual intercourse carries responsibility because it always involves the possibility of pregnancy. That possibility is part of the reason traditional morality and Christianity teach that sex should take place only within marriage, a stable relationship between a man and a woman in which a child can be cared for.[45]

Those who find instant pleasure in sex without the worry of children scoff at this reasoning. That is why contraception and abortion have permitted us to become a sexually permissive society governed by our own desires.

Finally, we must look at the feminist movement which advocates abortion. Feminists wanted equal rights with men and believe that bearing children is not their privilege, but rather a bane on their person that restricts their desire to compete with men. Foh states: "The feminist argument for abortion is phrased as the right of a woman to control her own body or her own reproduction."[46] She points out that when women control their own reproduction, they can escape the possibility of pregnancy and pursue careers in order to become independent.[47] "Without the opportunity to obtain an abortion when she does not want motherhood, a woman's freedom to guide her own fate does not exist."[48] Mary Ledbetter, past president of Feminists for Life, explains, "The inequalities women experience in society are factors in their seeking abortion."[49]

Seeking to avenge themselves through abortion, feminists become their own victims. For these women we must feel pity because they have missed the beauty of womanhood and all the privileges that are uniquely ours when we live as God intends.

It is *natural* for a woman to want to "be somebody." The feminists haven't discovered something new, they have merely voiced what many of us may not consciously realize. The problem with the feminists' approach is that rather than dealing with their wrong desires, they angrily force themselves into situations where they degrade themselves by debasing the womanhood they seek to elevate.

Feminists diligently have pushed *their* ideas of "ideal" womanhood in such a way that it *seems* we are missing something by becoming "keepers at home." There is nothing "wrong" with becoming a mother—God made women to bear children and raise them for His glory—the highest privilege accorded a person. Men have been denied the joy feminists now say women don't want.

Part of the beauty of being a woman is that God has endowed us with wonderful emotions which cause us to naturally nurture our children. God gave these emotions to us because He intends for us to bear children and knew we would need special grace to get us through the sometimes difficult months of pregnancy. Our problem is that we have followed the loud voices of a few who would push our natural tendencies to nurture into the background as they watch us rush to claim our rights.

The woman who is pregnant finds herself caught amidst the loudly voiced reasons, which are subtly seeking to use her for their own hidden motives, and her own quiet conscience. Faced with an untimely pregnancy, she thinks she sees acceptance and concern for her problem and foolishly allows the pro-abortionist to solve her problem for her. But a woman is easily deceived and often confuses "need" with "want" as she lets people who do not truly care for her direct her path.

Abortion was legalized so that the few women who believe pregnancy and childbearing to be repugnant could rid themselves of their problems without fear of legal reprisal. What has happened is that women who never would have aborted or even considered abortion are having abortions because they are now legally available.

When our government said we could not legally abort, the vast majority of us accepted it and went on with our pregnancies, bearing our children, and nurturing them into adulthood. My research shows that 83 percent of the women responding to my questionnaire who aborted legally, would not have aborted had it been illegal. There will always be some who think themselves desperate enough to go above the law to obtain an abortion. In a few instances, as with abortion, these people will manage to have the laws changed to their way of thinking.

Most of us did not consider abortion as an option before abortion-on-demand was available. Has our thinking really changed regarding abortion, or have we merely gone with the tide in doing the "accepted" thing?

FIVE

Acquiescently Aborted

No one goes through this ordeal for the sake of societal gain. No one is here to reduce the population growth. A given fetus lives or dies as the mother's needs dictate.[1]

Though Magda Denes, the woman who penned those words, advocates abortion, she has captured the truth that though millions of women have taken advantage of their legal right to abort, each individual woman has ultimately aborted for intensely personal reasons.

Knowing my own personal reasons for aborting, I was interested to know why other women chose abortion, and also their reactions prior to and following their decision.

However, though it had been thirteen years since my abortion, I personally knew only one other woman who had aborted. And as I endeavored to circulate my questionnaire (see Appendix B), I discovered that in spite of the fact that over 18 million women have aborted in the past thirteen years, finding them is not an easy task. The reason is simple—women who have experienced abortion rarely discuss their act publicly and usually hesitate to discuss their abortions privately, swearing their confidantes to secrecy.

In my search for women who have had one or more abortions, I spoke to a variety of people—physicians, psychologists, post-abortion counselors, ministers, friends, and strangers, most of whom were hesitant to contact aborted women they knew. Some of these sources later told me that when presented with the questionnaires, the women said they *wanted* to respond but could not face thinking about their abortions, as they would be required to do when answering the survey questions. In addition, I sent questionnaires directly to women whom I had been told had either had an abortion or knew someone who had one. In all cases, the women were requested to respond anonymously.

The questionnaire consisted of twenty-four specific questions regarding the abortion experience, with a twenty-fifth question inviting women to share additional comments with me. Many women did share their thoughts with me and I was both surprised and encouraged by their responses. In total, I received forty-six completed questionnaires from twenty states. Here, then, is the data I collected regarding forty-six women and why they chose abortion.

Women completing the questionnaire aborted between the ages of 15–34, with 89 percent aborting between the ages of 18–25. The average age at the time of the abortion was twenty-one. Most women (thirty-five) had only one abortion, but five women aborted twice; four women aborted three times; one woman had four abortions and one five, for a total of sixty-six abortions among forty-six women. Fifty-four abortions (82 percent) were done at twelve weeks gestation or less.

Of the sixty-six abortions, fifty-three were legal and thirteen were illegal. Forty were performed when the women were single; twenty-three while married; two while divorced; and one woman was separated at the time she aborted. Presently, thirty-nine women are married and one is divorced (as a direct result of her abortion); the remaining six are single.

Nine women had children prior to their abortions. Of these nine, six women had at least one child born since the abortion. Two women have healthy living children who survived a botched abortion procedure. In addition to these, nineteen women (41 percent) who had no children prior to their abortions, now have one or more living children. Two women of the forty-six *know* they are now sterile. Unknowingly, they killed the only children they would ever have.

At the time of their abortions, twenty-five women were denominational Protestants; eleven Catholic; three born-again Christians; one had a cultic background; two were atheists; and four stated they had no religious training prior to their abortions.

When asked, "Would you consent to another abortion?" forty-one women (89 percent) answered "NO!" Three women an swered yes; one said she did not know; and one did not respond. When asked, "Do you believe what you did was wrong?" forty-one women responded "yes" and five said "no." One woman who said she would not consent to another abortion nonetheless felt she did not do wrong; one woman who would consent to another abortion at the same time admitted she had done wrong. The other two women who said they would consent to another abortion, the one who did not know what she would do, and the one who did not respond to that question all believed they were not wrong in aborting.

The length of time since the abortions ranged from forty-three years to one and a half weeks prior to the response on the questionnaire, with most women (75 percent) having had their abortions 5–16 years ago. The average length of time since the abortion was nine years.

When asked about the specific reasons for their abortions, the women responded:

Reason for Abortion	Number of Abortions
Didn't want parents, husband, etc. to know	13
Told to abort by parents, husband, boyfriend	10
Strongly encouraged to abort by parents, husband, clinic	10
Not ready for parenting	8
Inconvenient time to have a baby	6
Selfishness	4
Felt it was only way out	3
Financial reasons	3
Bad marriage	2
Single	2
Didn't know	2
In school	1
Possible deformity from drugs	1
Unspecified health reasons	1
	66 total abortions

As you can see, thirty-three abortion decisions (50 percent) resulted from relationships with parents, boyfriends, or others—

either to protect or to please them. The women in these cases did not really want abortions, but had them nonetheless. Dr. Koop says, "It is obvious from some studies available that legal abortion is still a loathsome thing to many women who seek one."[2] Some of the women responded:

"Husband didn't want child, threatened divorce."

"Husband forced a choice—him or baby. Couldn't handle it."

"Ex-husband refused to believe it was his; I was afraid for myself and the child."

"Doctor encouraged us to because my husband was a student and I was having nausea and vomiting (later I found out this to be normal for pregnant women). Doctor called us at home; I didn't even think of abortion till the doctor highly recommended it."

"The father of the child was married and didn't want me to have the baby—I had no means to raise the child."

"Desire to protect family."

"My boyfriend, his parents, and my parents insisted it was the ONLY solution and wouldn't support any other alternative. I was all alone."

"I got the abortion mainly out of fear of my father finding out and his hurt in finding me pregnant."

"Was talked into it, practically forced [by] parents, boyfriend, doctor, counselors at abortion clinic."

"Fear—of shaming parents and self, coping with child, deformity in baby because of drugs I'd taken, parents, friends, and my doctor all influenced me to have an abortion."

"I had been afraid to tell my parents."

While we cannot condone the actions of these women, we should ask ourselves what would their decisions have been had one caring person encouraged them to carry their babies to term?

In contrast to these responses, let's look at some other women's explanations for their abortions:

> "I was divorced with two small children and embarrassed at having been caught in my sin of adultery. My motives were very selfish."

> "I was a *very* irresponsible 19-year-old. If anyone *willingly* took over being responsible for me, especially when I'd made a mess of things, I'd *willingly* choose to let them."

> "Money."

> "Having a baby just didn't fit into my life then."

> "Too young, no job, not ready to accept responsibility."

> "Conceived in an affair."

> "Not married."

> "Was not ready for parenting."

> "Not 'ready' for family."

> "Didn't want to have a child out of wedlock."

Some women aborted to protect or please someone else and others aborted simply because it suited their own purposes. Neither group fought to remain pregnant. Jill Lessard, quoted in "WEBA: Voice of Experience Relates Horrors of Abortion," sums it up this way: "An unwanted pregnancy presents such turmoil and inner conflict that a woman can't think clearly. She's apt to go along with what's expedient and convenient."[3]

When a woman finds herself faced with an untimely pregnancy, she tends to focus on the problem rather than on seeking a solution. Though aware that she is carrying life, albeit unborn, she conveniently closes that door of her mind. The woman's concern for the unborn baby is nonexistent or false concern at best.

Previously we learned that in the early months of pregnancy a woman is emotionally unstable due to hormonal changes taking place within her body. She is in no position to make a life-changing decision. Yet as David Granfield says, "If she is to make the decision, she must do it at the time when she is mentally least capable of doing so."[4] R.F.R. Gardner adds, "The pregnant woman, drugged as she is with hormones, is in no fit state to decide objectively. The very existence of the abortion option has magnified her difficulties."[5] Yet it is in the early months of pregnancy that most abortion decisions are made because that is when most abortions occur.

As we have seen, sometimes the woman has "assistance" with her decision, but frequently she does not. Regardless of whether she has consulted someone, ultimately each woman must decide on her own. But once the decision has been made and the abortion performed, there is no turning back. Women who have aborted lament time and again—*if only I had known, if only someone had told me the facts, if only I had listened, if only. . . .*

What We Didn't Understand

Unfortunately, compassion and wise counsel are often not available to the woman facing an untimely pregnancy. The seeming necessity for secrecy poses a barrier to proper information as the woman goes off to an abortion clinic for advice.

Though no woman should be pressured into having an abortion, we have seen that abortion is big business. Physicians who perform abortions by and large do not do what they do for the good of the woman. They do it for money.[6]

The abortionist has found a way to make big bucks quickly and legally. Do you honestly believe he would take the time to patiently inform his potential customers in a quiet and calm manner of the risks involved to her life and health? Of course not! His customers would desert in favor of self-preservation. When a woman truly *understands* what it takes to keep herself (and her baby) healthy and alive, she will usually do so.

> The statistics show that between 80 and 85 percent of the women who become informed about abortion and the abortion procedures and the development of their fetuses choose not to have an abortion, even after they have already decided it was the only alternative.[7]

It is *avoidance* of knowledge and *lack* of understanding that causes the woman to inflict harm upon herself and her unborn child.

Sometimes abortionists go about exerting pressure subtly by making the baby seem the culprit—"It will ruin your life." In other cases direct pressure is applied:

> I was pressured by the clinic. I called them—you don't have much time; you are twelve weeks along—come in tomorrow. Pressure was intense on me to decide quickly. Due to lack of support, lack of knowledge of a birthright or such *I decided* to have an abortion (quoted from a questionnaire).

No one can deny, least of all the woman who has aborted, that the "decision" was hers. But even when she changes her mind at the last minute, she is sometimes ignored:

> I have, however, experienced personally as well as heard of many instances where if the woman changes her mind while on the abortion table—she is *not* permitted to leave. This is a grave violation! (quoted from a questionnaire)

But most women do not change their minds at the last minute—once committed they go through with their plans. Part of the reason is that information regarding abortion procedures was never made clear to them when they were considering an abortion. I realize that the following descriptions may be traumatic for those of you who have aborted, but they are presented so that people may understand what abortion procedures involve, for though readily available, the information is not widely circulated.

There are several methods used to abort a baby. Prior to my abortion, these methods and their risks were not explained to me, nor did I have the common sense to ask. I was never told anything about the physiology and anatomy of the life in my womb, or that it could feel pain. Maybe I didn't want to know, but I wish someone had "forced" the following facts on me.

Up to twelve weeks gestation, a dilatation and curettage (D & C) can be performed with some degree of safety (to the mother). The cervix is forced open and an instrument shaped like a serrated spoon called a curette is used to scrape the baby off the wall of the uterus. Often discernible body parts are extracted.

Suction or vacuum extraction is also used during the first trimester (first three months). After dilating the cervix, a hollow plastic tube is inserted into the womb through the vagina. This method dismembers the baby by strong suction. The remains pass through the tube to a waiting container. A D & C may be used in conjunction with the suction to cut the baby into pieces for easier removal. Forceps may be needed to crush the baby's head if it is too large. Following the abortion, medical personnel often piece together the baby's parts to make certain it was all removed.

In these two methods, the doctor works only by touch. It is blind surgery. Perforation of the uterus and profuse bleeding are not uncommon in D & C's; the suction method can cause the need for blood transfusions as well.

Saline-induced abortions are most commonly used between the sixteenth and twenty-fourth weeks of pregnancy. The saline surrounds and is swallowed by the baby, who thrashes in a death struggle that can last up to an hour, sometimes longer. A physician describes a little-mentioned incident that may occur during saline induction:

> It happens that there is another little thing which I've never read about or discussed with anyone else. But on a number of occasions with the needle, I have harpooned the fetus. I can feel the fetus move at the end of the needle just like you have a fish hooked on a line. . . . You know that there is something alive in there that you're killing.[8]

In addition, the baby's skin is burned off by the saline solution. Though times vary, dead babies are usually expelled within forty-eight hours. The majority of these babies are born dead, but some have managed to survive.

The risk in a saline-induced abortion is greater for the woman than in the previous procedures. Should the doctor pierce one of the woman's veins, serious complications and even death could occur.

Another procedure, a hysterotomy, is often used for late abortions in the second and third trimesters. It can be legally performed until the time of delivery. This procedure is identical to a cesarean section, yet a hysterotomy is used to kill the baby, while a cesarean section saves the baby's life in a complicated delivery.

Hysterotomy abortions often result in living babies. The babies may be left to die of neglect or may be disposed of while still breathing:

> The incision was made into the abdomen, then into the uterus, and a baby was pulled out; I mean a fully developed, moving, breathing baby. . . . The baby was put into a bucket of water and drowned.[9]

Some of the babies surviving hysterotomies have mercifully been permitted to live. Some states, such as Pennsylvania, require a team of neonatal experts on hand at an hysterotomy abortion in case the baby is aborted alive. How ironic that some babies should defeat the purpose for which the surgery was intended.

There are other physical risks to the woman aborting in addition to those already described. Even people who favor abortion admit that abortion does carry risks, which are usually presented as being insignificant in comparison with continuing an untimely pregnancy. Corsaro and Korzeniowsky in their book, *A Woman's Guide to Safe Abortion*, state that one in twenty women experience a minor complication due to an abortion, a 5 percent risk, and that infection and incomplete abortions are the most common complications.[10] In reality, the figure is closer to 25 percent.[11] In a chapter titled, "Can Anything Go Wrong?" Corsaro and Korzeniowsky cover these risks:

> There is about a one-in-a-thousand chance that during the abortion, one of the instruments will pierce the uterus. . . . There is a slightly greater chance of perforation when a woman has general anesthesia, because the uterus is softer and more easily pierced. . . . The cervix can also be injured . . . tearing. . . . In very unusual circumstances, more serious injury can occur. A large tear can cause heavy bleeding, leading to shock. Or other organs may even be punctured . . . blood transfusion, surgery, or whatever [may be required]. . . . An abortion of any kind, at any time, may in some way damage the lining of the uterus, which

would affect future pregnancies. . . . Abortions performed later in the pregnancy . . . extensive cervical
dilation has been related to miscarriage and to births of
premature and underweight babies.[12]

The fact that these risks are listed in a book which strongly
advocates abortion, tells us that these must be bona fide risks.

Sterility can also result from an abortion. When a D & C re-
moves too much of the normal lining tissue of the uterus, and the
uterine cavity becomes scarred, this scarring interferes with fertility. Sterility is a high price to pay for deciding to "wait" to have
children.

Other complications are cited, such as increased menstrual
loss and painful intercourse.[13] Tubal (ectopic) pregnancies in-
crease in risk from 0.5 percent for all pregnancies to 3.9 percent
following abortion.[14]

Abortions are particularly dangerous for a first pregnancy. The
uterus of a woman who has never been pregnant is small. In a
pregnant woman the uterus grows with the baby; as it does the
cervix muscles get stronger. When the doctor expands the cervix for a D & C by inserting rings or tubes of gradually increasing
size, the muscles are spread apart so that the baby can be removed. Since the uterus has not had an opportunity to enlarge,
the cervical muscles have not strengthened. There is a good
chance they may be permanently weakened by forcing them
open. If this weakening occurs, and the woman becomes pregnant with a "timely" baby, the muscles may not be strong enough
to hold the baby—hence a miscarriage. In cases of lesser weakening of the muscles, a baby may be born alive but premature.

After repeated abortions a woman is two times more likely to
miscarry, have a premature birth, stillbirth, or difficult delivery.

On the other side of the coin are the complications which
affect the aborted women emotionally. At the January 1971 Cali-
fornia Abortion Symposium Dr. Paul Marx reported: "Doubts,
fears, anxiety, ambivalence, and guilt feelings characterize nearly
all abortion patients, the panelists generally agreed."[15]

Even so, prior to abortions, psychological risks are down-
played and often not considered by the woman nor mentioned
by the doctor. This is unfortunate, for as one woman stated on
her questionnaire:

> I have often read that aborted women suffer no emo-
> tional consequences and those that do are not emo-
> tionally strong anyway. Please help to stop this myth.
> Let people know if they had killed their baby they
> would be having a hard time dealing with it too.

On those occasions when psychological problems *are* discussed, it is often with the assumption that the abortion will eliminate those problems. Lippis says, "The most common reason
given for abortion is mental health (mental duress), yet abortion
will not cure any known mental illness and has proven to *often*
be psychologically harmful to the mother" [italics added].[16]

Another risk which is seldom mentioned, but which can result
from the adverse psychological impact of an abortion, is suicide.
Dr. Willke states:

> Most well-informed counselors in the profession are of
> the opinion that there are probably more suicides re-
> sulting from guilt and emotional upset *because* or from
> abortion than there are among women who cannot
> obtain an abortion [italics added].[17]

I truly believe that if prior to abortion women were shown
pictures of unborn babies at various stages of development, if we
were told in detail of the abortion procedures and the cruelty
inflicted on the baby, if we were informed of the risks to ourselves, we would in most instances reconsider. I can't help wondering how many children would be alive today and how many
women would not now be suffering needlessly if explicit information had been provided beforehand.

Regretful Reflections
The following quotations are from women who have aborted
one or more babies:

> "I feel frustration about the lack of information given to
> women in the position of deciding to abort. I have
> strong convictions about abortion now . . . my feel-
> ings when abortions are discussed are usually 'I want to
> help them understand that it isn't anything but murder.'
> Any other rationalization isn't the *truth*."

"I pray that we can turn the laws around to make abortion illegal. I know they still went on when it was illegal but not as much as now, and that's all it would have taken to save my baby—I wouldn't have had a leg to stand on. My parents wouldn't have wanted me to do something illegal . . . after the abortion you feel emptiness when you see people pregnant or with babies, and you feel a little pain and sadness. But after you have your own children, you HAVE to face up to what you had done when you had the abortion. It stares you in the face every time you look at your children and realize you could have had another dear blessing. Like I keep thinking, that I could have had a child in school this year. There's still pain."

"I know that abortion is killing and I would give anything to have the child now. I felt at the time that there was no other way, but there was. I am remembering a terrible time in my life—a time that I wish I could change. I could have raised a child at nineteen years old. It would have been difficult, but not impossible."

"I realize now what I didn't know then—that it would be the brutal killing of an innocent human being. Even if I didn't plan to have a baby, I never had the right to kill it."

"I always think that if only someone had suggested keeping the baby, I would have or if I had received any counseling maybe I wouldn't have gone through with it—I never considered doing anything else. The father of the baby is now my husband and when I think of that baby as a person it really hurts—she (or he) would have been eight this year."

"Abortion is *NOT* the answer to unplanned pregnancy. This is demonstrated clearly (aside from the scientific evidence that abortion *is* murder) by the traumatic aftermath both physical and emotional which scar the second victim in this monstrous act—the would-be mother."

"I have not met one woman who has not been affected in some way by her abortion. Many may try to deny their abortion has affected them as I did for many years, but abortion is not a single act that ends when the baby dies. Its aftermath is far-reaching."

"At the time I made the decision I felt there was nothing wrong with the issue of abortion, *I* believed what I was told about it, and moral issues weren't one of my higher priorities or I wouldn't have gotten pregnant in the first place. I had a fear before the abortion, but why I don't know. I felt relief afterwards, a sense of peace, my mistake was covered. But now I know the errs [sic] of abortion and the mistake of taking living and dying out of the hands of our Lord."

"When I went to the abortion clinic they said, 'Motherhood is selfish! It's an ego trip!' 'You need this abortion to get on with your life—to get into a career, school, to get somewhere.' Well, I had enough years to mull their words over in my mind and there are only certain conclusions a sane person can logically come to if they buy those lines: 'If motherhood is selfish, then so is fatherhood—logically speaking—and if that is so then these bums and scoundrels who desert their families are really saints, are really virtuous!'"

Even a woman who believes abortion is right says:

"I felt I did right because I couldn't care for a child. I was not willing to carry a child for nine months and then have to give it up. The thought of killing the child crossed my mind often and still does—but I did what I thought was right at the time. Even now sometimes I wonder if it was a boy or a girl or where I would be if I would have kept the child."

Can you relate to these women's words? I can, and if you have had an abortion you probably can too. Although we aborted for reasons which at the time seemed "right," our selfish motives produced harm to us. Unknown numbers of women suffer emotional and physical trauma which may last for years, sometimes for life. Actions done out of selfish motives eventually lead not to blessing, but to a curse upon the person doing the act.

When all is said and done, we must again come to the fact that abortion wasn't chosen because we felt it was right, but because we felt we had the right to choose. And though most of us know now that abortion is wrong, at the moment of decision we gave our consent.

Running Scared

Why did we consent to abortion? That we had doubts beforehand cannot be denied. Over one third of the women surveyed expressed having doubts *before* as well as *after* their abortions. We realize now that we lacked information, concern, and wise counsel. But what made us either ignore or avoid discovering the truth before it was too late? Can we find a common motive underlying each individual abortion decision? I believe we can.

Whether the reason be finances, family size, marital status, urging by family or friends, the basis for the abortion choice is always fear. In fact, 85 percent of the women responding to the questionnaire said they were afraid prior to their abortions, often stressing, "I was *deathly* afraid." Lippis says, "Abortion is contrary to all that life is; reflecting our ignorance and fear."[18] We were so afraid to tell parents or husbands; afraid we couldn't support a child; afraid our marriages would fail; afraid we'd have to drop out of school or give up a career; afraid our lives wouldn't continue as we had planned them; we took what we believed was the easy way out.

In my own case, I knew what I was doing was wrong even though practical and emotional support and proper information were lacking. But I felt trapped. Before abortion-on-demand was legalized, I would have carried my baby to term and raised him, but now I was faced with another option—the legal "right" to abort. I kept thinking about this option until it loomed so large as to preclude other choices. Abortion soon became the *only* solution. And so I ran scared, basing my choice on what the government said it was permissible to do—fleeing in terror from a future I couldn't know to a present that would not let me forget.

Gardner speaks to this:

> [Abortion] is a lifebuoy thrown to a drowning woman.
> The point to grasp is that it is the existence of this

lifebuoy that makes all the difference. The mother does
not now *have* to bend her back to this new burden with
such strength and courage as she can muster. Were
there no other outlet she would in all probability do
just that, and succeed in some measure. But given this
new option, that task assumes a terror and a dread di-
mension it never had before.[19]

Why couldn't we see that our fear had us exactly where so
many proponents of abortion claim we ought not to be? We were
not free to choose while imprisoned by our fears. Women rush to
abort because we have been scared to death. We were told it was
safe, OK, the best way for all concerned—and we permitted ourselves to believe what we were told. The situation we found ourselves in ruled our lives. Paralyzed by fear of the unknown future,
we rushed blindly to do that which was an immediate remedy, a
visible solution to our problems. Our choice became limited to
escaping that which frightened us—an untimely pregnancy. We
ignored the fact that we did not truly know what was involved in
our decision:

> She cannot know if there will be any operative compli-
> cation, and whether she will ever again be able to con-
> ceive. She cannot be sure how the other members of
> her family will react. She cannot know what will be the
> response of her own conscience post-operatively and
> in later life. No one can know.[20]

In spite of this, we were encouraged to run for our lives, forget-
ting anyone or anything else—just run, run, run!
And we ran—blind, frightened—unaware of or ignoring the
reality of what we were doing.

> They said it was okay to abort my small son;
> But afterward when I understood what I'd done
> My heart cried in anguish, O God, bring him back.
> But some things can't be undone; that's the sad fact.
>
> No judge will ever condemn what I've done—
> In court my case I would surely have won;
> For I had my life to live, the "right" to be free.
> I never considered anyone 'cept for me.

Yes, I regret the day I made my choice—
After all, of we two, I had the voice
To be heard across this land loud and clear.
But I ran to abort in the midst of my fear.

One moment in time to retrieve, this I pray,
But I can't have him back for I killed him that day.
Oh how could I allow this to happen to me
Now all that remains is my "right" to be free.

SIX

Actions Analyzed

No chapter in this book has been as difficult for me to write as this one. Perhaps the reason is that in analyzing the actions of women who have aborted, I am forced to scrutinize my own actions all over again. My natural tendency is to refuse to think about what actually occurred when I aborted, for in examining the evidence I expose myself to all the facts my mind wants to ignore. I may not have liked what I did, may not have really wanted to do it, but the fact is I *did* abort, and now certain questions confront me as I analyze: Was it life—human life—that grew in my womb? If life, was it murder to end that life? Did I have the right to do with my body as I pleased? Was it the child I didn't want or was it the responsibility or the pregnancy I fled? Did I value my situation in life more highly than I valued life itself? And finally, was the choice to abort ever mine to make?

Semantic Antics

Our choice of words and their phrasing play a vital role in determining how others interpret what we say. We can convey the same idea using different words and each time the message alters in the mind of the hearer or reader. By using words cunningly, we can make people believe we say something other than what we mean.

For example, consider the terminology used when referring to abortion. Years ago we heard of *therapeutic* abortions (for health reasons) and *criminal* abortions (for non-health reasons). Those two terms are simple, easy to understand. They meant that one could not obtain an abortion legally unless there was a clear indication that the woman's life or physical health was endangered.

Then came a new terminology—*indicated* versus *elective*. Indicated abortions are those where sufficient danger to the woman exists to warrant sacrificing the baby's life. Elective abortions are those chosen for personal reasons.

Today there are still two types of abortions—indicated and elective. But we have so refined our terminology that they are divided into six categories:

Therapeutic	Done for the sake of the mother's physical health or to save her life
Psychiatric (sometimes referred to as therapeutic)	Done for the mother's mental health
Eugenic	Performed to keep retarded or deformed children from being born
Social	Performed to ease economic pressure on a family
Ethical (or humanitarian)	Done in cases of rape or incest
On demand	Done for any reason

In order to clarify matters, I suggest we classify all abortions as either *needed* (to save the woman's life) or *wanted* (for all other reasons) since that is what our laws today warrant. We have seen that *very few* abortions are performed out of need (though we may choose to think we "needed" to abort). That leaves millions of abortions falling under the category of *wanted*.

Now we may say, "I *needed* the abortion because I didn't *want* a baby." What we are really saying is, "I *wanted* an abortion because I didn't *need* a baby." But those particular words don't sound humane, so now the terminology gets very tricky as we attempt to disguise our actions into appearing to be something they are not. We find ourselves saying, "Out of fairness to 'it' and to me, the fetus was aborted because it wasn't wanted." Or we may say, "The product of conception was terminated (or if you prefer, the uterine contents were removed) due to the fact that my socioeconomic circumstances warranted it because everyone has a right to control her own body and have the best life has to offer." This statement seemingly shows due concern for the "product of conception" who assumedly would suffer for being born in less than utopian conditions and for "me" because the status quo in my life must remain unaltered.

As if this were not enough, we are then challenged that the fetus is not a person. Don't let this confuse you because persons don't have to be people! For instance, a corporation can legally be considered a person. *Webster's Dictionary* defines a person as: "A human being; especially as designated from a thing or lower animal; individual man, woman, or child; a living human body; bodily form or appearances." What then are people? Again we turn to the dictionary which lists people as "human beings; as distinct from other animals." Both persons and people are listed as "human beings." A human being is "(1) of or characteristic of a person or persons; such as people have; (2) having the form or nature of a person; that is a person; consisting of people; (3) having or showing the qualities characteristic of people; a person usually a *human being.*"

We've come full circle—a person is a human being and a human being is one that has the characteristics of people, which in turn are human beings. Thus, if a human being is a people and a person is a human being, a people must be a person. But we are made to focus on the word *person* rather than on its synonym, "human being." As we shall see later in this chapter, semantics plays a vital role in determining what we do with the contents of our wombs.

Is it any wonder people are confused about what it is a woman carries in her womb and whether removing it is wrong?

Fetal Misconceptions

When Justice Blackmun, speaking for the Supreme Court in handing down the *Roe vs. Wade* decision, stated: "We need not resolve the difficult question of when life begins," he opened the door to the abortion clinics for millions of women.

But Justice Blackmun erred in his now historic statement. Ample proof exists (and existed in 1973 when the decision was made) that life begins at conception.

However, proponents of abortion, ignoring the facts, have seized upon Justice Blackmun's statement. An example of this is

Betty Benjamin's statement in her article, "The Case for Pro-Choice":

> Since life itself is a continuum, to argue about precisely "when life begins" during fetal development is to pursue an exercise in futility. Opponents of abortion base their case upon the premise that personhood begins when sperm meets egg. Rather, in the true scientific sense, an embryo or fetus is comparable to a set of blueprints up to the state of independent viability.[1]

First, to say that "to argue precisely when life begins during fetal development is to pursue an exercise in futility" is not a subject open to debate at all if one faces the facts. Biologists generally agree when a sperm from a human male fertilizes the egg from a human female, conception has occurred and it is at this point that life begins. A new human being has been created, having all the genetic ingredients that make him or her a unique individual.[2] Dr. Willke states:

> Nothing will be added to this being between the moment of fertilization and its ultimate death as an old man except time, nutrition, and oxygen. It is all there in toto at that moment, merely not fully developed.[3]

Science has merely "discovered" what God has already told us. "Before I formed thee in the belly I knew thee" (Jer. 1:5). Keil and Delitzsch, Old Testament commentators, explain: "God in His counsel has not only foreordained our life and being, but has predetermined before our birth what is to be our calling upon this earth; and He has accordingly so influenced our origin and growth in the womb, as to prepare us for what we are to become."[4]

Some argue that life begins at implantation (when the fertilized egg attaches itself to the wall of the uterus) a few days following conception. Dr. Shettles answers this argument: "Implantation . . . defines a condition by which life is *maintained* once it has already started."[5] [italics added]

But Dick Hafer presents an unarguable answer to the statement "no one can be sure when life begins." He says, "That answers itself. If no one knows, how dare one kill a baby that *may* be alive?"[6]

President Ronald Reagan speaks to this when he says:

> I have often said that when we talk about abortion, we are talking about two lives—the life of the mother and the life of the unborn child. Why else do we call a pregnant woman a mother? I have also said that anyone who doesn't feel sure whether we are talking about a second human life should clearly give life the benefit of the doubt. If you don't know whether a body is alive or dead, you would never bury it. I think this consideration itself should be enough for all of us to insist on protecting the unborn.[7]

To the statement that "an embryo or fetus is comparable to a set of blueprints," Dr. Willke comments:

> The blueprint of your home is merely the plans for your home. After using this instruction sheet to build your house, you can throw the blueprint away. It has not become the house. The fertilized ovum, soon called a zygote, is not the blueprint but is in fact the house in miniature. It itself will grow into the house in time. It is, in toto, the house already. Your home was built piece by piece and ultimately assumed a shape that could be identified as a house. The being that was to develop into the adult person you are, was totally here from the moment of conception. All you needed to become the adult you are was nutrition, oxygen, and time.[8]

Again Hafer sums it up well: "The fetus *grows* into an adult. A blueprint is *not* a building."[9]

A woman responding to the questionnaire did not mince words:

> I now believe as soon as the egg and the sperm connect life begins. It could be no other way if it were not true and the embryo then was not *alive* it would simply not grow, *that fact* that this tiny egg does grow means it *has* life and if it has life we certainly cannot say because it cannot walk or talk that it is dead. It is insane what the majority of the female population has bought, simply because they don't want to behave themselves morally.

And grow it does! At twenty-five days after conception, a tiny heart begins to beat; at four weeks, the entire nervous system is present and the tiny being's unique fingerprints have formed; at forty-three days, brain waves can be measured and his arms and legs move; at seven weeks, he weighs 1/30 of an ounce but has external features readily recognized as "human" and has all the internal organs of an adult; at sixty-three days, the pre-born child can grasp something placed in its hand and can make a fist—the new life is growing.

When lay people misrepresent facts, we can understand they may speak out of ignorance. But Dr. Shettles states:

> Even some pro-abortion scientists refer to the fetus [during all three trimesters], as "a mass of cells" or "mere tissue," in efforts to justify not only abortion, but even also experimentation on the unborn. Some . . . are willing to overlook the biological facts, convinced that abortion is an acceptable means to a desired end.[10]

Faced with the evidence for life beginning at conception, the pro-abortionist now grasps at straws: "But is a fertilized egg really a human being, or does it harbor only the *potential* of one?"[11] Dr. Shettles explains it this way:

> There is another argument sometimes raised by pro-abortionists that should be dealt with here. The fact that a significant number of zygotes fail to implant and therefore do not result in pregnancy is seized upon by a few as "evidence" that "even Mother Nature" does not consider the fertilized egg genuine human life, any more than "she" does the hundreds of thousands of eggs and millions of sperm that are "wasted." To this I can only answer that there are also a significant number of one-year-old infants who will never make it to old age, to puberty, or even to their second birthday. Does the fact that life is interrupted at some point after it has begun mean that it never existed?[12]

Granfield adds:

> If we judge merely by appearances, it is not difficult to refuse to a three-day-old morula [solid mass of cells

formed by ovum in early stage of development] the title, dignity, and rights of a human being. Yet appearances are often misleading, and to depend solely on appearance would be scientifically most unsophisticated.[13]

Lippis presents a good summary to the medical evidence:

> We can easily understand [from the scientific evidence] that there is no essential difference between the fertilized ovum *we all once were*, the embryo, fetus, infant, adolescent and adult. They are only stages of development for the same person. The fetus is not merely a "potential" human being, who is magically "switched on" to personhood at birth; rather, he is a unique individual, alive and active, aware of his environment, and developing faster than he will ever again.[14]

Thus, when someone asks, "Is the newly conceived being the same as you or I?" you can respond that indeed you are not the "same" as you were yesterday. Your chemical makeup changes daily: new cells replace old ones and hair falls out. You are not the same moment by moment, much less from conception to adulthood. But you are the same person that was once inside your mother's womb. Changing as you are, you never changed your genetic makeup.

But Clifford Bajema hits the nail on the head with his statement: "But is it human life? . . . I might ask: 'what other choice is there?' It certainly isn't zebra life or azalea life."[15]

By abortion we short-circuit God's plan for the tiny human being. Not only do we admit that the child is worthless in our own eyes, but we assume he would be worthless to God. But this human being is of inestimable value in the eyes of God. God created man in His own image (Gen. 1:26-27) and gave to him intellect, ability to reason, and freedom to choose. This is what makes us different from all other living creatures. God cared for each of us personally even before we were conceived:

> For Thou didst form my inward parts; Thou didst weave me in my mother's womb. I will give thanks to Thee, for I am fearfully and wonderfully made; wonder-

ful are Thy works, and my soul knows it very well. My frame was not hidden from Thee, when I was made in secret, and skillfully wrought in the depths of the earth. Thine eyes have seen my unformed substance; and in Thy book they were all written, the days that were ordained for me, when as yet there was not one of them (Ps. 139:13-16).

How God must love us to care for us so. And notice that it is God who ordains the length of our lives.

Furthermore, God does not differentiate between unborn and newly born children. They are both referred to by the Greek word *brephos*, which means "an unborn child, embryo, fetus; a newborn child, an infant, a babe."[16] Instances of the use of *brephos* include Luke 1:41, 44 where we find an *unborn child* leaping in his mother's womb for joy. In Luke 2:12, 16 newborn Jesus is called a *brephos*. In Luke 18:15-17 *infants* were brought to Jesus to touch. Acts 7:19 refers to *children* between the ages of birth and two.

The references in the Gospel of Luke are particularly important because they clearly show that "Dr. Luke, medically trained and inspired by the Holy Spirit, makes no distinction between born and unborn children."[17]

Further biblical proof of the unborn baby being a human comes from Psalms: "Surely I have been a sinner from birth, sinful from the time my mother conceived me" (Ps. 51:5, NIV). Dr. Charles Ryrie says this "establishes the humanness of the fetus since guilt is attached to it and since only humans and angels can be guilty of sin."[18]

Regardless of the proof that a fetus is a living, developing human being, the Supreme Court determined that legal personhood does not exist prenatally. Therefore, an unborn child became divested of his right to legal protection under the law. Yet we are not allowed to kill an eagle or to break its egg. Why? Because we expect the egg will eventually hatch, producing another eagle, and eagles are rare. Why then is it we are not allowed to kill a born person, but are allowed to remove "uterine contents"? Logically, we could expect a human being to eventually emerge from an undisturbed womb. The answer is simple— human life is not valued highly because human beings are plentiful.

Prior to 1973 unborn children could sue for damages, inherit property, and collect Social Security benefits. But because an unborn child has been designated a nonperson by the 1973 Court decision, *legally* he can be denied the rights guaranteed to all people under the 14th Amendment: "Nor shall any state deprive any person of life, liberty, or property without due process of law, nor deny to any person within its jurisdiction that equal protection of the law."

By declaring the unborn to be nonpersons, not only are they denied property, liberty, and their very lives, but they are no longer entitled to due process of law which might save them. "In 1857 the Court's decision was based on skin color. Today it is literally on the basis of living environment, for as long as the child lives in the womb, he or she can be killed by abortion."[19]

Bajema gives us food for thought: "Are we ready to concede that the question of when human personhood begins is purely a matter of *definition*, not of *fact*?"[20]

Viability

Another method for sanctioning abortion is to establish viability, which means "able to live; at that stage of development that will permit it to live and develop under normal conditions, outside of the uterus." The context here is vital. Legally, viability has come to mean the baby is capable of living *on its own* outside the womb. The very consideration of viability assumes we are dealing with something which already *lives*, but is presently dependent on another for its continued life.

Are any of us *truly* "viable"? Certainly very few of us, even as adults, are capable of surviving "on our own." Consider particularly the newborn baby—though he is breathing, kicking, and screaming, he is not viable according to the legal definition of the term. If left to himself, he will surely die. Viability apparently has a great deal to do with *how* one comes to be outside the womb.

In 1973 the Supreme Court placed viability at twenty-eight weeks, but conceded it could occur earlier. In 1970 New York State had placed the limit at twenty-four weeks. Dr. Nathanson tells how that date was determined:

> I had the opportunity to ask Assemblywoman Constance Cook about how the architects of the bill had arrived at the twenty-four-week limit. She told me, a

little apologetically, that doctors regarded the twentieth week as that point at which the expulsion is no longer an abortion but a premature delivery, and the fetus is an "infant" born alive, or a "stillbirth" if born dead. The older English common law figured viability, the point at which a prematurely delivered fetus had a reasonable chance to survive, at twenty-eight weeks. At this point in her exegesis she paused a beat or two, then said: "We split the difference." And that, children, is how the laws are written.[21]

Magda Denes puts it this way:

> Extrauterine viability of the fetus as a deciding factor in doing abortions is a position of ignorance or of extreme bad faith.
>
> Abortion fetuses, after all, come to be outside the uterus by force and not by mishap. To argue, therefore, in favor of abortion exclusively on the basis of viability is logically akin to maintaining that to drown a nonswimmer in a bathtub is all right, because he would have drowned anyway had he fallen into the ocean.[22]

The age at which viability is set is a matter of life and death. If it is determined the fetus can't survive outside the womb, an unborn baby's mother may abort him without cause, the premise being he would have died anyway. If he has become viable, there is at least a slim chance he may be allowed to live. But something that has been sadly ignored is that with the advances in medical science, the age of viability gets lower and lower. It is clear that we permit viable fetuses to be aborted. A woman shares with us:

> I see many "preemie" babies that weigh 1-2-3 lbs. and they use every available means of equipment and spare no cost in keeping that child alive, but in the instance of an unwanted child it can be terminated now upon its natural delivery date. How can on one hand [one] fight so hard to save a tiny infant's life and on the other hand care so little to save it? Only because *the* child is *unwanted*, because it is inconvenient for whatever the reasons the child's death simply is based upon the inop-

portune time of its existence. (Quoted from a question-naire)

Is It Murder?

There now remains one question to resolve in our examination of misconceptions regarding the life of the fetus and that is, *Is abortion murder?*

God prohibits murder. Exodus 20:13 clearly states, "You shall not murder," as does Romans 13:9. Exodus 21:22–23 addresses the issue of a non-spontaneous abortion.

> And if men struggle with each other and strike a woman with child so that she has a miscarriage, yet there is no further injury, he shall surely be fined as the woman's husband may demand of him; and he shall pay as the judges decide. But if there is any further injury, then you shall appoint as a penalty life for life.

I understand this passage to mean that if a pregnant woman is struck during the course of two men fighting and the baby is born prematurely but alive ("no further injury"), the penalty is a fine which the husband imposes for the premature delivery. If, however, the baby is aborted or dies ("further injury"), God exacts the death penalty. This is the same penalty God commands for murder (Gen. 9:6).

Since God has given the death penalty as punishment if the child dies, we know He equates the murder of unborn children with the murder of already born people.

As if it were not enough that abortion is murder in the eyes of God, America has declared murder to be wrong legally as well. We have been told that abortion is not illegal and is therefore not murder. The dictionary tells us that to kill is simply to put to death, to destroy life in any way. Since life begins at conception, we can hardly deny that abortion is killing. But murder is the unlawful and malicious or premeditated killing of one human being by another; it is to kill inhumanely or barbariously.

The film, *The Silent Scream,* shows a ten-week-old unborn child aborted by suction. I quote from an article in *Last Days Newsletter:*

> At first you see the child at play, sucking his thumb and moving about. But at the *very* moment the suction tip

touches the amniotic sac you see the child *jump* away
and move to the top of the uterus as though he senses
something aggressive is happening. His mouth opens in
a silent scream and you can see his heart speed up and
his arms and legs moving rapidly. Then you see the suction tube tearing away first one arm and then the other,
as the child writhes in pain. You see the spinal column
slipping down the tube until only the baby's head is left
with a piece of spine on it. And finally you see the abortionist searching for the baby's head.[23]

May God forgive us. Regardless of what man's law says, can you
honestly believe that the fetus is not a human being and that
taking its life in such a way is anything less than murder?

Is It Ever OK?

We now come to the question, *Is abortion ever OK?* Immediately, Bethany leaps to my mind. Bethany is adorable with big
brown eyes and a smile that will melt your heart. She is happy,
bright, and as active as any normal three-year-old. When you
meet Bethany for the first time, you may be shocked to notice
that her left hand is little more than a stump. Bethany was born
deformed. No one but God knows why. Yet had her mother
known of this deformity prior to her birth, Bethany's mom could
have aborted her. Surely Bethany's "quality of life" may differ
from that of a person who has two hands, but her love of life and
desire to live are no less than yours or mine.

With modern technology we can often detect abnormalities in
a developing baby. Amniocentesis can be done at approximately
fourteen weeks and can detect physical abnormalities as well as
potential mental defects. Norman Anderson comments in *Issues
of Life and Death*:

> If reverence for human life must prevent us from put-
> ting an imbecile to death, or deliberately sacrificing the
> life of a defective baby which has already been
> born . . . then are not much the same principles appli-
> cable to the destruction of a fetus which is already in an
> advanced state of development?[24]

In spite of the fact that errors can be made in determining
defects prior to birth, many women abort because they believe

the lives of their deformed children would be a waste. But we never can be certain that even if born handicapped in some way, the person himself would consider his life a waste.

The fact that God would permit a deformed or retarded child to be born rather than spontaneously miscarry tells us that God has a purpose for that child. Though the child may be expendable in our eyes, his very existence affects others for God's purposes. Bill Shade relates this story in *How to Commit Murder and Make It Legal*:

> I shall never forget the first time that I was in Johnny's room and saw him lying there in his crib with a large adult head attached to a deformed and spindly body that might have belonged to a five-year-old. On inquiry I learned that Johnny was in fact 41 years of age and had been deformed from the time of birth. He was born completely helpless and had remained in [his mother's] continual care during the entire period of 41 years. Johnny was incapable of any meaningful communication, although he did smile and respond to his mother when she attended him and from time to time he would feebly attempt a few elementary words. He had never sat up, but had lain like that on a bed all these years. . . .
>
> Johnny's condition was the result of a forcible rape that had taken place during pregnancy. Johnny's mother had [been attacked and struck] . . . on the head with a hard wooden object, knocking her unconscious and opening an immense wound that bled profusely. [Her attacker] then raped her and fled, leaving her on the kitchen floor in a pool of blood.
>
> She was not rescued until the next day when 27 stitches were required to sew up her scalp at the hospital. She told me, "The baby didn't move very much after it happened."
>
> When Johnny was born, he was crippled and deformed; but when I asked her if she felt that abortion would have been a better solution, she reacted violently.
>
> "No," she said. "You see God used Johnny to show me how to deal with people. They come here for coun-

seling and after they see Johnny, they feel that they
don't really have a problem and if I can accept God's
grace to deal with my problems, surely they can accept
His grace to face whatever theirs may be. . . . When
people come to me with similar problems, I counsel
them to keep their children. Johnny has given me more
than I have ever given him."

Before I left she said, "I don't have a care in the world
for I know before God that I have done right."[25]

A person may be born handicapped "so that the works of God
might be displayed" in his life (John 9:3). God made each of us
the way we are. "And the Lord said to [Moses], 'Who has made
man's mouth? Or who makes him dumb or deaf, or seeing or
blind? Is it not I, the Lord?'" (Ex. 4:11) God never makes mistakes.

Hafer responds to the problem of what to do about unborn
children we know to be deformed: "Since when is perfection a
qualification for life? If so, in unborn babies, why not in humans
already born?"[26] Hafer's second question brings up a subject that
is becoming accepted. If we can choose to kill a defective child
before birth, what is wrong with killing one that "slipped by" our
detection and was born defective?

The bottom line from a human standpoint is this: Who is to
decide what defects are severe enough to warrant the death penalty before (or following) birth?

Another area where there is genuine concern whether abortion is permissible is in cases of rape. Pregnancy resulting from
rape is rare. Statistics indicate approximately 3 percent of the
women raped become pregnant.

I think Dr. Shettles offers the best counsel when pregnancy
does result from rape or incest:

> I believe that a rational and compassionate society
> should offer the victim encouragement—physical, psy-
> chological, and financial—to carry her baby to term.[27]

A woman pregnant by rape does not need the trauma of abortion
added to her troubled mind.

We must remember that as in all cases of pregnancy, the baby is
innocent. He came to be in the womb through no fault of his
own. For a rape victim to seek revenge by extinguishing an inno-

cent life will solve nothing. Children are *not* to be put to death for the sins of their fathers (Deut. 24:16).

I understand that carrying the baby may present emotional trauma and inconvenience, but a woman in this situation must focus her attention on the fact that the baby is also *her* own flesh and blood: she is his mother. A woman viewing the unborn child from this vantage point might very well come to love him even before his birth. If at birth she truly does not want the child, she may place him for adoption; but if she considers the baby as hers, she may very well choose to keep him.

Melody Green asks this question: "Think about this: If you found out tomorrow that you were the product of rape—would you wish that your mother had aborted you?"[28]

In summary, Dr. Shettle's conclusion is correct:

> Abortion does nothing to right the grievous wrong of rape or incest; indeed, it only compounds it, adding to the assault of one innocent person the taking of the life of another innocent person.[29]

Finally, we must consider whether abortion should be performed in cases where the mother is seriously ill.

Rarely today does the mother's condition warrant abortion. Though the mother may be sick, she most often can carry her baby to term or viability. In those cases in which it is believed a woman would die unless the pregnancy were terminated, the baby is sacrificed. Questions, however, arise:

- In how many instances do we know *for a fact* that the mother *will* die unless the baby is aborted?
- What guarantee do we have that if the baby is aborted, the mother's life will continue?

Perhaps the mother would have died anyway and the tiny life that was sacrificed for her benefit could have lived for years. Who is to know?

A case in point exists. A woman in her late twenties has cancer, was given one to two years to live, then became pregnant. Doctors urged her to abort in order to prolong her life. This woman chose to continue to carry her baby. In the meantime, the cancer has gone into remission and the child was born healthy. How would that woman feel today if she had aborted that child?

Every woman giving birth faces the possibility of death even in the best circumstances. Who can ever know prior to birth what the outcome will be?

Life can end at any point in its cycle from conception to death of old age; only God knows when it has been appointed for each of us to die. I believe that God in His wisdom permits a woman's body to spontaneously miscarry in those instances when, for reasons often unknown to us, an unborn baby's life is foreordained to end prior to birth. "Man's days are determined; You [God] have decreed the number of his months and have set limits he cannot exceed" (Job 14:5, NIV). "All the days ordained for me were written in Your book before one of them came to be" (Ps. 139:16, NIV).

As the owner of all life, God gives us children as a gift and a reward (Isa. 8:18; Ps. 127:3-4). Notice that God does not say some children are gifts and others are not. Each child is a gift and is to be received as such. God never says we may reject a child, and indeed considers it a curse for a child to be born prematurely. Furthermore, we have no right to question why God makes a person as He chooses. "But who are you, O man, to talk back to God? Shall what is formed say to him who formed it, 'Why did you make me like this?'" (Rom. 9:20, NIV).

God owns all life: "The earth is the Lord's, and all it contains, the world, and all those who dwell in it" (Ps. 24:1). Every person is formed as God permits. He makes no mistakes.

Fatal Mistake

In earlier chapters I've alluded to the woman's belief that she has the right to control her own body; and that particularly in the area of reproduction, "controlling her own body" allows a woman the freedom to "be equal with men."

The simple fact is that we cannot totally control our bodies. For instance, we have little control over whether our bodies become sick or diseased; we cannot control what someone else may do to our bodies; and once we engage in sexual intercourse, we cannot control our reproductive system.

What we *can* control, however, is whether *we* take the risk that enables our bodies to become pregnant (except in the case of rape). There is a word that would end millions of abortions before they even were considered. This word shows *we* are in control of our bodies, rather than our bodies being in control of us; that word is "no!" "No" to sexual intercourse other than with one's husband.

Why do you suppose God so sternly forbids sexual intercourse outside of marriage? Look at His words:

> You shall not commit adultery (Ex. 20:14; also refer to Deut. 5:18; Matt. 5:27; 19:18; Mark 10:19; Luke 18:20).

> Abstain from . . . fornication (Acts 15:20, 29).

> For this is the will of God, your sanctification; that is, that you abstain from sexual immorality (1 Thes. 4:3).

> Let marriage be held in honor among all, and let the marriage bed be undefiled; for fornicators and adulterers God will judge (Heb. 13:4).

Sex is reserved for marriage for two reasons: (1) the union created by two people physically joining is a picture of Christ and His church (Christians);[30] and (2) God created people so that when they become one flesh physically, the possibility of propagation exists. In other words, a baby might result from the act of sexual intercourse. Like it or not, that is the fact and all our methods of contraception can never totally guarantee that conception will not occur.

If pregnancy occurs, it is the beginning of a new and separate life. The words "it's my body" ignore the fact that with pregnancy we are dealing with not one, but *two* bodies. But since only one body has the ability to cast a vote, the woman always wins.

Medical science has proven that the "contents" of a pregnant woman's uterus are *not* part of her body, though the two bodies are *connected* by the placenta.

> Functionally, the placenta is a blood pool, a two-way transfer point. There is a biochemical exchange between mother and child: Blood is the medium, the umbilical cord is the channel, the placenta is the mechanism, and nutrition, respiration, excretion, and protection are the purposes. . . . But there is no intermingling of blood. The proverbial sharing of blood

between mother and child is a biological myth. Mother and child have separate blood supplies and circulation.[31]

Bajema states: "The mere fact of attachment does not make the child part of the mother anymore than a car becomes part of a gas pump to which it is attached for fueling purposes."[32] The unborn child is a person residing within a person. That the developing child is totally dependent upon his mother for all of his needs from conception until he is mature enough to survive in the world outside the womb is not the same as saying "it is part of the mother's body." The baby is not a parasite nor part of the woman's tissue. He has a separate body which today can be tested and even operated upon within the womb; his tiny body can also be removed from the womb. And upon removal what is found? A separate body with all its own systems. Garton states: "Abortion, by any logical, biological, or theological standard is, at the very least, the destruction of a separate human body."[33]

Herbert Vander Lugt sums it up well in his booklet, *A Matter of Life and Death*: "The right of a woman to have control over her own body doesn't extend to the fetus because it is not part of her body."[34]

But do women have the right to treat unborn children as intruders into their wombs? Bajema clarifies the question as he asks: "Is it an intruder or does it have a right to be in the womb—residing there by an act apart from its own willful involvement?"[35] I like James Townsend's conclusion:

> The woman's body is her own, by gift of God, until she engages in activity that invites a guest to share it with her for a period of time, roughly nine months. Having entered into that solemn obligation, she is bound by the law of God and nature not to disturb the tenant. She has a property right in her body and she, for a consideration, voluntarily [except in rape] relinquished a part of that right to another. Her body is no longer completely her own. That is what pregnancy means.[36]

The life that is in the womb didn't ask to be there, didn't get there on its own, but now being placed in that position, wants desperately to remain there, sheltered by his mother. God has given the woman's body as protection for the unborn child; she is a "caretaker" for the new life. God views a pregnancy that fails to result in live birth as a curse (Ps. 58:8; Hosea 9:14; 13:16); and a baby being removed violently from the womb as a horrendous occurrence causing great sorrow (2 Kings 8:12; 15:16). Amos 1:13 speaks of judgment upon those causing the premature death. Therefore, morally, it falls upon the woman to do everything possible to protect the life in her womb.

"He Had a Right to Be Wanted"
Having worked through the fact that life begins at conception, that this life is not part of a woman's body to dispose of as she pleases, and that abortion is rarely, if ever "OK," we now find ourselves saying, "But I only did what was best for the baby. He had a *right* to be wanted."

Dr. Harold O. J. Brown says,

> Human beings, since time began, have realized that children are a lot of trouble. Our society tells us, by supporting abortion on demand, that children are *not* worth the trouble. Logically that applies to wanted children as well as unwanted ones, and so the result is that fewer and fewer children are being wanted.[37]

Since the woman doesn't want the baby, we are told, he will be abused and battered, unnurtured or deprived. I admit that seeing abused, neglected children is heartbreaking, but what is to guarantee this will happen if a woman carried her baby to term when she would rather abort?[38] The truth of the matter is that "abortion is the first violence a child can experience at the hands of an adult."[39]

A pregnant woman who begins to consider whether she wants her baby is using hindsight to determine something that should have been considered prior to having sexual intercourse.

I believe God gives a woman nine months in order to prepare her heart for the task ahead. It's not as though one day a woman is pregnant and the next day a baby emerges. It normally takes nine months and we can wisely use that time to accept the gift, however untimely, that God has for us. "If a woman allows normal and natural maternal instincts to take control of her mind and feelings during the time of pregnancy, she will begin gradually to want the baby forming inside her body."[40]

The real issue is not that the child is unwanted, but that the pregnancy is untimely or unwanted. The Group for the Advancement of Psychiatry, which supports abortion, presents this case for unwantedness:

> It is an attitude compounded of dismay, frustration, and anger; it is the attitude of the woman whose baby represented blasted hopes and ruined plans, lost chances and missed opportunities, dropping out of school and rushing into precipitous, ill-considered marriage. It afflicts unwed teenage mothers and middle-aged mothers ready to turn to other things; it permeates whole families under stress of increased family size, decreased family resources, and the endless unhappy consequences of one life too many. This "unwanting" is too well grounded to be dissolved by the charm of a new baby.[41]

They sum up well the feelings of a woman faced with an untimely pregnancy. This *is* how we feel. But they err in their final assessment, for regardless of our circumstances, we can still learn to *want* this new life so inconveniently thrust upon us by our own actions. It is *our attitude* we must change.

What about Adoption?

Sometimes it is suggested that the woman might give her baby up for adoption following its birth. This is not a method of forcing women to have babies for infertile couples, as some proponents of abortion would have us believe, but rather a sort of compromise in an effort to save the life of the baby while at the same time freeing the woman from the responsibilities of motherhood.

One reason I chose to abort was because I could not bear the thought of carrying my baby for nine months only to relinquish him. That sounds inhumane, I realize now. But to me the problem wasn't the baby; the problem was the pregnancy. I wasn't prepared to be pregnant. Had I gotten through those nine months, I would gladly have kept the child, but I couldn't see past the pregnancy to the actuality of giving birth. Pregnancy and baby were two entirely different things in my mind. Therefore, when someone suggested adoption, I recoiled in fear of losing the baby and began considering aborting the pregnancy.

Gardner relates that my feelings are not uncommon as he quotes an American psychiatrist, Dr. Rosen:

> "No one in the technical literature has stressed the heartlessness, the cruelty and the sadism that the pregnant woman so frequently senses—perhaps correctly, perhaps mistakenly—when the physician, minister, or lawyer suggests to her that she carry the child to term and then hand it over, never to see it again, to someone else to rear. They object to 'farming the child out for adoption' and maintain 'I'm not an animal. Do you think I could give away my baby after carrying it for nine months?'" . . . Rosen continues that during the past eighteen years he had seen only three patients for whom "farming out" of a child for adoption would not have been emotionally exceedingly traumatic and psychiatrically contraindicated. For some twenty-nine patients who came into psychiatric treatment within one to four years after they had accepted this kind of recommendation (which they considered to be the abandoning of their infants), all but seven required extensive therapeutic management. A woman does not lightly leave a baby on someone else's doorstep, or even in a hospital nursery.[42]

The National Abortion Rights Action League in "20 Myths About Abortion," states, "No woman should be forced to bear a child only to give it up for adoption. Psychologically, giving up a child is far more traumatic than having an early abortion. Married couples find it impossible to give up unwanted children.[43]

If women can be "forced" to bear their children, they seldom give them up. This negates the traumas of abortion or adoption. Ninety-six percent of unmarried women who can be convinced to carry their babies to term realize at birth that they really *are* mothers and keep their children.[44]

And what of the women who aborted because they didn't *want* to be pregnant? As we have seen, many women now regret their actions, realizing *wantedness* was an attitude of their own choosing.

Those few women who do decide to place their babies for adoption can be assured he is wanted:

Actually, the "unwanted baby" is a myth. There is no such thing. Due to shortages of newborn babies for adoption, there are thousands of couples who long night and day to hold and love the children so many mothers are throwing away. Those who say they are getting an abortion for the sake of their "unwanted child" are obviously not thinking of the *child's* happiness and well-being . . . but of their own.[45]

The "New" Ethic

We learned earlier that fear motivates an abortion. But what is it women fear and why do we fear it to the point of destroying our lives and those of our babies?

The woman who submits to an abortion may not be aware of moving from one philosophy of human life to another. Probably the religious and philosophical implications of it all are not very clear to her. But by her action she has moved from the large camp of those who think all human life has value and is worth protecting to the smaller but growing camp of those who think its value is dependent on other things—its "meaningfulness" or "wantedness."[46]

That statement was written nine years ago and since then the "camp" of those holding to the sanctity of life has dwindled as the "camp" of those advocating the quality of life has grown, encompassing unwary people in its ranks. The "old" ethic, which holds all human life to be of intrinsic worth and of equal value, has been subtly replaced by a venemous snake which has slyly slithered its way into our midst. This "new" ethic "purports to seek the greatest good for the greatest number, even if that means some individuals must suffer or die in the public interest."[47]

The sanctity of life or old ethic, is based in Christianity and views man as finite in capabilities and infinite in his worth. The quality of life or new ethic is based in secular humanism and views man as finite in his worth but infinite in his capabilities.[48]

First of all, it is important to understand that this "new" ethic is not so very new. It has been around since man began and Cain decided to do what he wanted rather than what God told him to do. Since then this thinking has caused the downfall of every civilization it has permeated. Ancient Rome and Greece are prime examples. God warned if we continued in things omitting Him, He will turn us over to our own desires and let us cause our own destruction (Rom. 1:18-32). The term "new" ethic is a synonym for secular humanism. And secular humanism sounds good at first:

> We assert that humanism will: (a) affirm life rather than deny it; (b) seek to elicit the possibilities of life, not flee from it; and (c) endeavor to establish the conditions of a satisfactory life for all, not merely for the few.[49]

But as we read further, the *Humanist Manifesto II* has reassessed its earlier statements and added this:

> We affirm that moral values derive their source from human experience. Ethics is *autonomous* and situational. . . . Ethics stems from human needs and interest. To deny this distorts the whole basis of life. Human life has meaning because we create and develop our futures. . . . We strive for the good life, here and now. The goal is to pursue life's enrichment.[50]

Do you see it? The "satisfactory life for *all*" is based on situation ethics, which says there are no absolutes; something may be right or may be wrong at any given time, depending on the situation in which a given value is involved. In denying absolute right or wrong, the humanist denies the existence of God. In doing so, he believes he frees himself to act according to his own wishes without accountability to anyone else.

But the Bible tells us, "The fool has said in his heart, 'There is no God,' they are corrupt, and have committed abominable injustice; there is no one who does good" (Ps. 53:1). One of the abominable injustices the humanist has done is to permeate our society with the belief that abortion is "good." Claire Chambers in *The Siecus Circle* states, "The entire anti-abortion repeal movement has been a humanist enterprise from start to finish . . . this irrefutable fact is rarely revealed to the general public."[51] She goes on to cite cases and names (e.g., *Roe vs. Wade; Doe vs. Bolton*) where known humanists were influential. Chambers says that in 1966 The American Humanist Association passed a resolution in favor of elective abortion; in 1967 their top priority was abortion law reform. That same year Colorado became the first state to lessen legal barriers to abortion.[52]

Having researched the subject of abortion in-depth, I agree with Chambers' findings. Secular humanism *has* affected America's approach to abortion.

The *Humanist Manifesto II* continues: "The preciousness and dignity of the individual person is a central humanist value. . . . The right to . . . abortion . . . should be recognized."[53] To the humanist, life is valuable, but only insofar as it is valuable to any given person in any given situation. A humanist believes he has the right to determine that another life is of less value than his own. Therefore, a humanist recognizes abortion as an option at a point in time when the unborn person ceases to be valuable in his eyes. We can readily see that "abortion is the legitimate offspring of humanism."[54]

The secular humanist mindset says: We are entitled to judge the value of another's existence solely on what benefit we can derive from it. The humanist never considers the Golden Rule. He never thinks in terms of unconditional love for another human being; for that kind of love causes us to give of ourselves for the benefit of another. A humanist's love is conditional—if it's convenient, if it's compatible with what I want to do, and if it contributes to bettering my lifestyle, then I will love.

That is why women today abort their unborn children in order to pursue careers or finish school, to maintain the status quo of a relationship, or whatever their reasoning may be. Children in today's society take a backseat to the family car—after all, our quality of life would suffer without two cars. But if we have another baby, we can't afford two cars. Or, do we want to stay in this tiny apartment or do we want that house? We can't have a baby *and* a house—the baby wasn't in our plans and will have to go.

"To 'want' or 'not want' children is to dehumanize them."[55] The child then is seen as the property of the mother to be disposed of as her needs dictate. Rosalind Petchesky, author of *Abortion and Women's Choice*, says:

> We do have a moral obligation to nonpersons—to fetuses, animals, trees, and all organic life. . . . The problem is, of course, that the survival of these living things may conflict with some important rights and needs of

actual persons, and that in the face of such conflict, we must give priority to actual, conscious human beings over other forms of life."[56]

To this end, the humanist says:

I believe we have the responsibility to advocate the fetal right not to be born unless the physical, mental, emotional, and environmental well-being of its mother is assured.[57]

First of all, claiming the "fetal right not to be born" is a synonym for abortion. Realizing this, let us consider the following hypothetical case:

A woman is in tip-top physical shape, having no ailments of any kind. Mentally she is happy and content. Emotionally she is secure with a career and a loving husband. Her environment is perfect with a big house, cars, designer clothing, etc. This woman decides she wants a child since her well-being is assured. Therefore a baby now has the right to be born to her. She becomes pregnant and eventually delivers a bouncing baby boy. Suddenly an accident occurs and the woman is paralyzed from her neck to her toes for the rest of her life. Now her quality of life is drastically altered— physically, mentally, emotionally, and environmentally. She was not assured of her personal well-being as she had assumed. There now exists a baby who had the right not to be born—what do we do with him?

Others argue for the quality of life from the child's standpoint: "I argue that reproduction should be limited to those persons capable of endowing children with a reasonable chance to achieve happiness, self-sufficiency, good health, and good citizenship."[58] But who can know that the child conceived in less than utopian conditions might not be born into excellent circumstances?

La Fontaine states the error of these types of thinking:

Abortion proponents contend that under certain circumstances abortion is a merciful alternative to an otherwise wretched life. They refer to physical deformity, extreme poverty, and the likelihood of severe child abuse. This argument confuses the quality of life with life itself.

We reply that man has no authority to destroy life once it has begun. Man does not have the right to determine whose life is not worth living.[59]

Granfield states:

> The mother who wants an abortion because of the unborn child's foreseen defects or her own mental or physical or financial limitations is making her lethal decision on a false assumption: namely, that life with these defects or limitations is not worth living.[60]

Abortion to sustain our quality of life is the coward's way out. It is never as good nor as brave as having the child. When faced with the reality of what we are doing, can any reason to abort outweigh the fact that an unborn person, helpless and counting on you to sustain his life, will be murdered? What in life could possibly be worth taking your own child's life?

A woman's natural instinct is to nurture, to care for, to meet the needs of her offspring. Most of us who have aborted have found that having an education or a career, a big house or a car, freedom from responsibility, or whatever situation we based our choice upon, was not more important than raising the children God placed in our wombs. Too late we learned that the humanist philosophy is self-defeating because without children this world is going nowhere. Our precious children assure us there *will be* a future to strive toward.

The Final Analysis

Ideally, every child conceived should be wanted and loved, but though this criteria is often lacking, it does not grant a woman a bona fide reason to abort. We cannot force a person to love or want us and we cannot force a woman to love or want her baby. What each person does have a right to is continued life, which begins at conception. Each person, once conceived, has the right to be born if God so wills it. It matters not whether we are born into poverty or riches, sickness or health. God already knows the trials the unborn child will face as he takes his place in the world, and He intends to bring the child through this life for His own purposes.

How about you? Were your conditions at birth exactly as your parents desired? What if your mother had chosen to abort you? Aren't you glad she chose life for you? Wouldn't it be wonderful if all pregnant women were willing to make the sacrifices your mother did in order to give you life?

But millions of women engage in sexual intercourse with the full knowledge they will not have to bear their children should pregnancy occur. We who have aborted, whatever the reason, have short-changed ourselves of the blessing God intended to give through the child we destroyed. Instead of saying "Lord, help me to love this new life regardless of the circumstances of his conception," our attitude was "me first." We now realize that "abortion *creates its own need* by perpetuating a disregard for the unborn child."[61] This disregard for life is part of a "new" ethic which is very old. It says that each woman may do what is right in her own eyes at any given point in time, as long as her actions benefit her personally.

But in our humanistic mindset we failed to acknowledge that

> God alone has full and perfect dominion over others, the power of life and death. As the Creator of all men, He implements their individual right to life by His power and commandments: "The innocent and the just person thou shalt not put to death, because I abhor the wicked" (Ex. 23:7). God's superior authority over all men is the ultimate guarantee of the inalienability of the right to life, even in the womb.[62]

Did we ever have a choice? The answer is "no." But people have taken it upon themselves to condone the slaughter of innocent unborn children.

To this God says: "There is a way which seems right to a man, but its end is the way of death" (Prov. 14:12).

SEVEN

Accountability

Some women who have aborted their babies are able to go on with their lives, to all outward appearances, without conscious regard for what they have done. At some point these women may have felt afraid and even a little guilty because they aborted, but they pushed their feelings into the recesses of their minds and said, "I didn't do anything wrong—no one's going to put a guilt trip on me!"

Let's face it, denial is one of the best coping mechanisms we have. But I believe most women sooner or later live to regret having aborted.

Often "relief" is the immediate reaction of women who have aborted, and with good reasons: the pregnancy that was so undesirable, so unwanted, so *untimely* is gone. On the other hand, many women know at once they have killed their baby, crying as one woman did: "O God, I killed my baby, please forgive me." But it may be hours, days, weeks, or possibly years until the realization of what you have done begins to gnaw at your conscience, intruding into your life, refusing to let you live in peace.

Nora Scott Kinzer, author of *Stress and the American Woman*, believes

> Anyone who is morally or ethically or religiously or personally opposed to abortion, and anyone who believes that abortion is tantamount to murder will undoubtedly suffer guilt and psychological stress. But that is the very person who probably wouldn't have the abortion anyway.[1]

I disagree with Kinzer's statement, because I have found that women *do* abort despite their moral or religious beliefs, and regardless of whether they believe it is murder and are personally opposed to abortion. Women abort because they are scared, and all their other beliefs fade rapidly into the background as the women seek to alleviate that which frightens them.

Forty (87 percent) of the forty-six women responding to my questionnaire admitted feeling guilty at some time following their abortion, and seventeen listed guilt as an emotion prior to their abortion. As we saw earlier, these women came from a variety of religious backgrounds and personal beliefs regarding abortion. Some are no longer troubled with guilt, while others say, "My immediate response was relief—but that soon passed and all that I have ever felt since is guilt."

The question that we must now answer is—does feeling (or not feeling) guilty have any bearing on whether we are guilty in this matter of abortion?

The dictionary defines guilt as "the act or state of having done a wrong or committed an offense; culpability, legal or ethical; conduct that involves guilt; wrongdoing; crime; sin." That seems straightforward enough. Guilt follows wrongdoing. When one does wrong (sins), she then often *feels* guilty for the incorrect conduct. Guilty is defined as "having guilt; deserving blame or punishment; having one's guilt proved; showing or conscious of guilt; of or involving guilt or a sense of guilt." In other words, you feel guilty because of guilt in your life.

Proponents of abortion tell us that we who are opposed to abortion "force" our morals on others causing them to feel guilty. If we are so successful in "forcing" our beliefs onto others, why do 1.5 million women abort annually? Unfortunately, anti-abortionists have not been too successful in convincing women that what they are doing is wrong; for if we were successful, abortion would decline as women became aware of the guilt their act would bring upon themselves.

There must be another reason so many women feel guilty after, as well as before, their abortions.

Paul Marx quotes Freudian psychiatrist-obstetrician Julius Fogel from an article in the *Los Angeles Times*:

> I think every woman—whatever her age, her background, or sexuality—has a trauma at destroying a

pregnancy. A level of humanness is touched. This is a part of her own life. She destroys a pregnancy, she is destroying herself. There is no way it can be innocuous. One is dealing with the life force. It is totally beside the point whether or not you think a life is there. You cannot deny that something is being created and that this creation is physically happening. . . . Often the trauma may sink into the unconscious and never surface in the woman's lifetime. But it is not as harmless and casual an event as many in the pro-abortion crowd insist. A psychological price is paid, I can't say exactly what.[2]

Harold Brown gives a reason for such a reaction in women aborting:

> The Western world has held for 2,500 years that abortion is morally wrong. . . . Even many pagans who were advocates of sexual liberty . . . condemned abortion as murder. With the establishment of the Hippocratic Oath and the rise of Christianity, it came to be generally accepted that abortion is an atrocious crime.
>
> Orthodox Judaism, Roman Catholicism, and biblical Protestantism—which together include the majority of America's people—all teach that it is a very serious attack on a human being made in the image of God, and is a grievous sin.[3]

Brown continues by saying that because of our Judeo-Christian heritage, women in America are "going to have problems with guilt over an abortion."[4] This is true, but the guilt goes deeper still than our Judeo-Christian heritage. It goes to the very root of our being regardless of what we have been taught to believe.

> The belief that it [abortion] is wrong is so much a part of our culture that it will almost inevitably affect any woman who has one, regardless of what she thinks she believes about the morality of abortion.[5]

Richard Ganz goes a step further in seeking the reason why women who have had abortions feel guilt. He believes that the reason for guilt lies in the fact that moral laws are in themselves real and do not require our personal or collective acceptance or belief in them to exist. Guilt feelings

> may relate to the real transgression of a true moral law that exists independently of our belief in it or adherence to it. The guilt feeling may not be severe or permanent. But the guilt itself is.[6]

The problem is the act, not the guilt feeling. Even if you don't *feel* guilty, you are in fact guilty before God, for it is His moral law you have transgressed. "The problem is whether they are guilty not whether they feel guilty."[7]

A woman who carries a child in her womb cannot block the fact out of her mind, try as she may. Even though not always conscious of it, her mind mulls over what is happening inside of her body. Indeed, her body itself changes as a constant reminder of the newly formed life—menstrual periods cease, hair changes texture, breasts swell and may be sore, morning sickness begins, frequent urination—all signal that someone else is at least partially controlling certain bodily functions. These facts cannot be denied in the attempt to rationalize away the baby. A pregnant woman knows she is carrying a new life, whether or not she admits it to herself.

Understandably she would feel guilt when she decided to terminate her pregnancy, for with the pregnancy goes the unborn baby.

Dr. Willke answers the question, "Do these guilt feelings come from religious beliefs?"

> Certainly there are guilt feelings relating to religious beliefs, but most guilt feelings subsequent to abortion have little to do with sectarian religious belief. Abortion violates something very basic in a woman's nature. She normally is the giver of life. Most women who are pregnant are quite aware of the fact that they have a baby growing within them. Most women who have an abortion feel that they have killed their baby. Sometimes there is an almost irresolvable guilt, continuing self-reproach, and depression. . . . A wise psychiatrist has said that it is easier to scrape the baby out of the

mother's womb than to scrape the thought of that baby out of her mind.[8]

Whether the guilt feeling is temporary or permanent, whether it comes as a result of religious beliefs or from some deep inner knowledge, the fact remains that the woman *is* guilty whether she feels the guilt or not.

> The real problem is whether abortion *is* sin or murder. . . . Is it right? Men cannot determine the answer alone. . . . Discord, uncertainty, confusion, and anguish are the inevitable result of man's moral quest if he has no reference point outside himself.[9]

We have seen that if people go by what they think or believe to be right depending upon the situation, their conclusions may lead them to perform wrong acts, for by nature we do what is most expedient for us regardless of the effect on others. We also saw that God says abortion is equal to murder, which He forbids. Therefore, abortion is sin in the eyes of God.

It is no wonder that going to a psychiatrist (as many women do following their abortions) to alleviate your guilt has failed or at best worked only temporarily. Traditional psychiatry assumes there is no absolute standard of right and wrong; every situation is different. Helping a person to "feel" better, as traditional psychiatry does, only covers the truth of unresolved guilt. Your guilt will gradually creep back to attack you when you least expect it.

Ganz again comments:

> One wonders what kind of maturity the psychiatrists are promoting by encouraging a woman to deal with such a great responsibility by abandoning it and to resolve her conflicts about motherhood and ambivalence about childbearing by destroying her child . . . in the present pro-abortion climate, a woman who feels guilty and admits it to herself and others is opposing the most highly esteemed experts of the entire nation.[10]

Indeed, the Supreme Court, physicians, feminists, liberal churches, and others advocate abortion and tell you it's nothing to feel guilty about. Don't believe them! Guilt is not merely a feeling, but a conviction of your entire being that helps you know when an action you are about to do or have done is wrong.

Judy Miles in her pamphlet, "Love Letter to a Girl in Trouble," says:

> Well-meaning counselors often convince a girl that her guilty feelings about abortion are only because of faulty upbringing. But those guilty feelings are the urgent warnings of God's Holy Spirit in her conscience.[11]

How I wish someone had shared that with me fifteen years ago. Unfortunately, we women have too often pushed aside the guilty feelings we felt and rushed off to abort, only to find we should have heeded our guilt feelings before the guilt became fact.

And the guilt lingers, often for a long time. In researching this book, someone told me of a family friend in her seventies who had an abortion fifty-three years ago. To this very day, that woman cannot discuss the topic except to say, "I feel so guilty. Will God ever forgive me?"

Guilt does not come when there is nothing about which to feel guilty. No one has to make you feel guilty about having had an abortion. You are guilty whether or not you admit it to yourself, and you stand accountable to God for your actions. You may delude yourself into believing that God does not know, but the Bible says:

> For the Word of God is living and active and sharper than any two-edged sword, and piercing as far as the division of soul and spirit, of both joints and marrow, and able to judge the thoughts and intentions of the heart. And there is no creature hidden from His sight, but all things are open and laid bare to the eyes of Him with whom we have to do (Heb. 4:12-13).

You need to face the fact that you, by an act of your own free will, pronounced a death sentence upon another human being— you were not the executioner, but you surely were the judge. This admission of guilt is the first step in the healing process. By admitting you are guilty, you are saying, "I know I did something wrong; I feel bad about it. Now what can I do about it to rid myself of this burden of guilt?"

Most of us who aborted know we are guilty. It now becomes important for us to understand how to reconcile our guilt before God. Only then can the guilt be removed.

RESOLVING THE AFTERMATH

E I G H T

Acquittal Available

Abortion is not an issue that is going to one day fade away. Even if legislation once again forbids abortion-on-demand, millions of women have already committed that irrevocable act of abortion and now must live each day with a sin which is ever present before their eyes. Repeal of abortion-on-demand will come too late for these women.

Some women refuse to admit they have any emotional aftermath accompanying their abortion, blithely pushing that part of their lives into the recesses of their minds. But more women than are willing to admit—either to themselves or anyone else— struggle with their abortions in what appears to them to be a losing battle. These too may try to "shelve" their emotions. Unless abortion's aftermath is dealt with once and for all, it will continue to haunt the women who have had abortions.

It was not until five years following my abortion that I truly found the answer to my guilt. The privilege is mine to tell you how your guilt can be erased—totally, completely, and forever. You *can* find release from your fears, anger, grief, and depression which have resulted from your abortion. Sound wonderful? Something you're longing for? I hope you hate having had an abortion enough to grab the only lifeline that can save you.

Why We Need Acquittal

I wish I could look you in the eye and tell you that God loves *you!* Think of the person you love the very most on this earth—who is it? A friend? A family member? Now think how much you love that person. You'd do just about anything for him or her, right?

God loves you even *more* than that! God loves you no matter what you have done or what you will do. He loves you regardless of the fact that you aborted your unborn child. God will never stop loving you—never! And guess what? He wants to give you something very special—a gift—free and undeserved.

There are no strings attached to God's gift. However, there are some things you must understand in order to see why you should accept God's gift.

Each person one day will die. That is, our bodies will die. The Bible tells us there is a part of us that cannot die or be killed (Matt. 10:28). We call it our soul. After the physical body dies, that part of us which still lives, our soul, will be judged. "It is appointed for men to die once and after this comes judgment" (Heb. 9:27).

What is this judgment and why should we be concerned what happens to us after we die? The judgment determines whether God will grant or refuse us admittance into heaven. Since our souls live forever, we need to be concerned whether we will enter heaven when our physical bodies die.

Heaven is a glorious place! The Bible tells us that God lives there (Deut. 26:15; Ecc. 5:2; Matt. 6:9). Heaven is a happy place where no tears or pain exist (Rev. 21:4; Isa. 25:8). Heaven is a real place and God wishes to *give* the gift of eternal life in heaven to you and to me.

There is only one problem: all people are sinners.

> As it is written, there is none righteous, not even one; there is none who understands, there is none who seeks for God; all have turned aside, together they have become useless; There is none who does good, there is not even one (Rom. 3:10–12).

Every one of us has sinned (Rom. 3:23). What is sin? Sin is "missing the mark"—falling short of what God requires—in our thoughts, in our words, and in our actions. Sin is disobeying God.

Our natural tendency to sin is something we have inherited— every person on earth has inherited—from Adam, who committed the first sin in Eden as he and Eve ate the forbidden fruit (Gen. 3:1-7). By eating, they disobeyed God's command not to eat of the tree of the knowledge of good and evil. It seemed such a *little* sin, but because of that one sin, every person ever born also sins (Rom. 5:12).

But it's not enough to read that everyone has sinned. Sin is a personal act. You need to admit *you* are a sinner. In fact, if you say you don't sin, you deceive yourself (1 John 1:8). Unless you admit you sin, you won't see your need for God's gift and will miss out on the wonderful future God has planned for you. You will also remain burdened with guilt.

It is up to you to admit you sinned against God by participating in the destruction of an unborn person created in God's image. It doesn't matter whether you really wanted the abortion or not, the fact that you consented for your unborn baby to be removed from your womb "on demand" makes you a sinner. Probably you already knew you sinned when you aborted, but the truth of the matter is you sinned long before your abortion. Have you ever committed fornication? Ever lied or cheated? Ever lost your temper? Ever failed to do good to someone when you had the opportunity? God says each of these is sin against Him.

The Bible tells us that "the wages of sin is death" (Rom. 6:23). Because of sin we have earned death. This death is not merely physical death, but death in the sense of separation from God. In other words, we flunked God's test. "For whoever keeps the whole law and yet stumbles in one point, he has become guilty of all" (James 2:10). No matter how small your sin (or how large), it is enough to keep you separated from God.

Because God is holy and pure, He cannot tolerate sin. "Because it is written, 'You shall be holy, for I am holy'" (1 Peter 1:16). If God were only love, we could *all* go to heaven; if He were only just, we'd *all* have a problem—but God is both loving and just.

How can God keep loving us, judge our sin as He has sworn to do, and turn right around and offer us the gift of eternal life? God has solved the problem for us in the most amazing way!

A Gift for You

A woman asked me, "How can I ever atone for murder?"

The answer is simple: we can *never* atone for killing our babies, or for any other sin we have committed. However, *acquittal* is available to each of us. God now sees you as guilty of the sin of aborting your unborn child. There is a way that God can see you as not guilty of that same sin if only you will reach out by faith and grasp for dear life the lifeline that has been flung to you with precision and forethought. That lifeline is Jesus Christ—God's sacrifice for you and your means of entering heaven (John 1:29).

Jesus Christ, God before the world began (John 1:1) and crea-
tor of all things (Col. 1:16), humbled Himself and became a man
because of God's great love for us (Phil. 2:6-8). Born of a virgin
(Isa. 7:14; Matt. 1:23), conceived by the Holy Spirit (Matt. 1:20),
Jesus lived a sinless, perfect life on this earth. Though He was
tempted just as we are with sin, Christ *never* sinned (Heb. 4:15).
He was indeed perfect—and only perfection could bridge the
gap between us and a perfect God.

Christ was born to die that we might live, for without the shed-
ding of blood there is no forgiveness of sin (Heb. 9:22). Christ did
die, nearly 2,000 years ago, to pay the price of our sins (Isa. 53:6).
This was how God kept on loving us, but punished our sins—He
did it through His Son, Jesus Christ.

Eternal life is a *free* gift. However, the gift that is free to us was
not a "cheap" gift for the giver. My dear friend, the death Jesus
died was agonizing; the hours prior to His death were painful and
degrading. Betrayed by one of His closest associates, Jesus was
mocked, spit upon (Matt. 26:67), and scourged so that His face
was a bloody pulp (Isa. 52:14). Tried illegally and condemned
though found innocent, He was sentenced to die by a mad mob.
Then He dragged His weary body through the streets of Jerusa-
lem under the weight of a huge wooden cross. So weak was Jesus
that someone else was forced to carry the cross (Matt. 27:32).
Christ was nailed to His cross—a nail piercing each hand and
both feet. And then, with Christ's flesh quivering in agony from
the impact, the cross was righted and jammed with a resounding
thud into a pre-dug hole.

He hung there in pain as people continued to mock and blas-
pheme Him ("Come down if You can"). Crucified between two
thieves, Christ in His final moments on that cross became sin for
us (2 Cor. 5:21). Even God the Father turned away from Christ
for that moment (Matt. 27:46).

Christ then hung His head and voluntarily died for us. He did
not want to die (Matt. 26:39), but obeyed His Father's wish. Why
would Jesus, the perfect Son of God, die if He did not have to? The
answer is overwhelming when you realize what it means—
Christ died the most cruel, derisive death because He loves *you*.
"Greater love has no one than this, that one lay down his life for
his friends" (John 15:13). Yet we were *not* friends, but sinners
according to Romans 3:23, deserving of eternal separation from
God (Rom. 6:23). "But God demonstrates His own love toward

us, in that while we were yet sinners, Christ died for us" (5:8).

But dying was not enough. In order to make Christ's victory over sin and death complete, three days later God raised Him from the dead (1 Cor. 15:3-4). Christ continues to live, sitting at the right hand of God the Father in heaven (Heb. 1:3).

Accepting God's Gift

How can you receive the gift of eternal life that God offers? Each person comes to receive the gift of eternal life *individually* and that can only be done when you, *by faith alone*, trust the work Christ did on the cross as sufficient to cleanse you from your sins. Then and only then do you become a child of God (John 1:12).

"For by grace you have been saved through faith; and that not of yourselves, it is the gift of God; not as a result of works, that no one should boast" (Eph. 2:8-9). God's gift of eternal life is the only thing in life that is truly *free!*

The alternative to eternal life is eternal death, for until you become a child of God you remain in your sins and are separated from God. If you die without having accepted God's free gift of salvation through Christ's shed blood on your behalf, you will spend eternity in hell. Hell is also a real place and many people are going there because they reject God's gift of eternal life through Christ. God never *sends* anyone to hell—our own sin of unbelief sends us there. God always provides a way to heaven—simple faith takes us there.

Will you take God at His word that the atonement for your sin has been made and accept Christ's finished work on your behalf? Will you reach out and eagerly take God's free gift to you? "The free gift of God is eternal life in Christ Jesus our Lord" (Rom. 6:23; see also John 14:1-3). Jesus is "the way, and the truth, and the life; no one comes to the Father, but through [Him]" (John 14:6). "He saved us, not on the basis of deeds which we have done in righteousness" (Titus 3:5). It is only through God's grace, His unmerited favor, that we are rescued from sin. The means to obtain God's grace is simple faith—trusting Him to save us.

Aren't you longing to be free from the burden of guilt that weighs so heavily on you? "If you confess with your mouth Jesus as Lord [God], and believe in your heart that God raised Him from the dead, you shall be saved" (Rom. 10:9). Confess and believe—that's all. Then the innocent blood you shed through abortion will be washed from you and you will be whiter than snow. And there's something more—Christ's finished work on the cross removed *every* sin you ever committed or ever will commit! When Christ paid the bill, He paid it all!

Perhaps you want to accept Christ's gift of eternal life right now. You may tell God you accept His gift of salvation in words like these:

> Dear Heavenly Father,
> I want the gift of eternal life You offer freely through the finished work of Christ. I admit that I am a sinner and can do nothing to earn my way to heaven. I am sorry for my sins and with empty hands I come before You now to take the gift You freely offer me. By faith alone I accept Christ's death and resurrection as payment in full for my sins. Thank You for sending Christ to pay the penalty for my sin and for guaranteeing I will one day spend eternity with You. Amen.

There's More!

No matter what happens from this point on, if you have accepted Christ, your salvation is secure (John 10:27-29) and your sins are forgiven. But we may live many years on earth before we join God in heaven, so there is something else God has provided for us. We can have intimate fellowship with God right now through praise, prayer, and ministry to others. This concerns not our salvation from sin, but rather our separation from sin. Fellowship with God Almighty, whom Christians may call "Father," is contingent upon our dealing with our sins as they occur. Yes, we *still* sin (1 John 1:8) even though we don't want to (Rom. 7). God knows we will sin and that is why Christ's "paid in full" covers even our future sins.

God in His wisdom has provided a way for us to be cleansed daily from the guilt of sin—confession, not to a priest or other human, but directly to God. First John 1:9 promises, "If we confess our sins, He [God] is faithful and righteous to forgive us our sins and to cleanse us from all unrighteousness." Confession means to admit we are wrong. After admitting our sin, we then need to repent (turn away) from that which displeases God.

If you were a Christian at the time of your abortion, you know you have some matters to set right with God. Have you told God you are sorry for aborting your baby? Have you asked His forgiveness? Have you thanked Him for loving you in spite of your sins? You need to do this to keep your fellowship with God.

Can you ever atone for murder? No. But God, through Christ's substitutionary atonement, has forgiven you. David, who wrote many of the psalms, was an adulterer and a murderer. Here are his words:

> Bless the Lord, O my soul, and forget none of His bene-fits; who pardons *all* your iniquities; who heals all your diseases; who redeems your life from the pit; who crowns you with loving-kindness and compassion. . . . He has not dealt with us according to our sins, nor rewarded us according to our iniquities. For as high as the heavens are above the earth, so great is His loving-kindness toward those who fear Him. As far as the east is from the west, so far has He removed our transgressions from us. Just as a father has compassion on his children, so the Lord has compassion on those who fear Him (Ps. 103:2-4, 10-13).

Not only did David believe God could and would forgive him, he claimed God's forgiveness, appropriating it for himself. It does no good for us to be forgiven unless we *believe* we *are* forgiven and *act* as though we are forgiven.

God didn't send His only Son, the Lord Jesus Christ, to redeem you from your sins only to have you remain stifled beneath a ton of guilt, shame, and depression. Our God is greater than that. He wants to heal you from all your inner turmoil.

It's the Only Way
When women responded to my questionnaire, many surprised me by including comments regarding how they had resolved their inner conflicts resulting from their abortions. But I was not surprised to find that every woman who has come to terms with her act has done so through Jesus Christ. No other permanent solution was given for resolving the guilt and all the accompanying emotions. To encourage you, I include here some of the comments women shared with me:

> "[I am] forgiven and redeemed by Christ Jesus."

"God has healed my hurts. I just hurt for others going through this. Without the Lord, I would not be able to face what I did."

"Jesus Christ forgives and they [aborted women] can be very effective in dissuading others from going the selfish/abortion route."

"I am at peace through the forgiveness the Lord Jesus Christ has given me . . . total absolution through the shed blood of Jesus Christ is the answer for grieving women to be free from the past."

"Jesus has healed me and I forgave myself. The pain is an occasional reminder that I had a hurt but I can go on with the help of God."

"You can talk about it, cry, fellowship, go to shrinks, but without Jesus there is *NO* peace."

"I couldn't handle what I did. I had all the rotten feelings and I finally had to get before God and ask forgiveness for my ignorance and turn it over to Him. He did a supernatural work in me. Praise the Lord!"

"God is giving me peace about it all. He has comforted me and forgiven me."

"I just thank the Lord that He cared enough about me to save me. He is the only One who could forgive me for this sin. I hate to think where I'd be now were it not for Him."

God loves you so. He is in the business of taking broken lives and making them whole. Give God *all* the pieces of your shattered life and watch Him work a miracle in you!

NINE

Applying Atonement

If you have accepted Christ as your personal Saviour you may be disappointed to discover that all, or most, of your bad feelings which resulted from your abortion still remain. Or, it may be that you are suddenly experiencing unpleasant feelings for the very first time regarding your abortion. You are faced with the fact that God's gracious gift of salvation pardoned your sin, but did not release you from your merciless memories.

God has not extended salvation as an immediate cure-all for your problems. However, accepting Christ's payment for sin on your behalf assures you that your problems can be dealt with and resolved—that Christ Himself will assist you to come to terms with your abortion. "For we do not have a high priest who cannot sympathize with our weaknesses, but one who has been tempted in all things as we are, yet without sin. Let us therefore draw near with confidence to the throne of grace, that we may receive mercy and may find grace to help in time of need" (Heb. 4:15-16). Help is yours for the asking!

Perhaps you were a Christian at the time you aborted and have only now asked God's forgiveness. Seeking forgiveness does not solve your problems like some magic formula. It is likely that the emotions you are now experiencing—the guilt, grief, anger, or depression—have become a part of you, a result of improper thought patterns and actions before and following your abortion. In fact, as a Christian you have a sensitivity to right and wrong that may amplify your emotional turmoil.

Some of us have tried psychiatrists, physicians, and religion to alleviate our guilt, anger, and depression. As we have discovered, the methods of denial, withholding our feelings inside us, or brazenly talking about our abortions as if we didn't care, all worked for a time, but eventually our true feelings regarding our abortions resurfaced and have refused to go away. This is because there is no permanent solution to *any* problem we face outside of Jesus Christ. Only the Lord Himself has the answers we seek. And God has lovingly given us those answers in the Bible. That is where I finally went to resolve my own guilt, shame, depression, and bitterness. The Bible is where you too must go if you truly *want* to resolve your own emotional problems completely and permanently. The Bible was written for our instruction, that "through perseverence and the encouragement of the Scriptures we might have hope" (Rom. 15:4). You do not have to remain burdened with bad feelings and thoughts concerning your abortion.

You cannot, however, solve your emotional conflicts on your own, but only through the power of the Holy Spirit. The Holy Spirit is that part of God which came to live inside of you the moment you accepted Christ as your Saviour (2 Cor. 1:22; 5:5). The Holy Spirit will remain with you throughout your earthly life (John 14:16-17). However, there is a great difference between the Holy Spirit *residing* in you and *working* in you. He resides in each believer by *His* choice. He works through each believer by *our* choice. We can choose to draw upon His power or not. When we depend on the Holy Spirit to work in our lives through us, He controls our thoughts and actions in a way pleasing to God—but only as we *choose* to let Him (1 Thes. 5:19; Eph. 4:30).

A word of caution—don't try to work through your emotions on your own strength. You will fail miserably. Also, don't try to solve your problems so that you feel better personally. You must seek to resolve the turmoil in your life in order to please God and bring glory to Him.

When I came to know the Lord as my personal Saviour five years following my abortion, my life was a mess. My marriage was in shambles because I was emotionally unfaithful to my husband, pining for a man who neither loved nor wanted me; bitterness chipped away at my insides as I dwelled on the ones who had "helped" me in my decision to abort; grief lingered as I continued to mourn for my lost son; depression engulfed me as I focused on how miserable I felt; and shame kept me from getting the help I needed and later from making myself available to assist other women who have aborted.

Today I am free from the sins related to my abortion. God alone receives the glory for my new life—it took time for me to work through the emotional upheaval caused by my abortion, but I dealt with my problems through God's Word by the power of the Holy Spirit and He continues to keep me free from the horrendous emotions that once consumed me. Only an occasional memory remains to remind me that God's love and mercy are boundless to forgive so great a sin.

When there has been a terrible sin in our lives, such as abortion, the accompanying emotions can control our lives if we let them. Be assured that your problems are not unique and that they can be solved in God's way. "No temptation has overtaken you but such as is common to man; and God is faithful, who will not allow you to be tempted beyond what you are able, but with the temptation will provide the way of escape also, that you may be able to endure it" (1 Cor. 10:13). As you begin to work through your problems God's way, cling to those words and claim them as God's personal promise to you. Others *have* gone through what you are now going through, and you have God's assurance that He has not allowed anything to come into your life that He will not see you through. That's wonderful news!

The Bible tells us that when we are Christians, all things in our lives work for good as God molds us into the image of Christ (Rom. 8:28-29). God could simply "zap" us into conformity to the image of Christ, but He has chosen to mold us by means of testings encountered throughout life. Our responses to unpleasant circumstances are the means by which God causes us to grow in Christ. Every trial you are experiencing ultimately will be used to your benefit for God's glory. Hold on to that truth. You probably do not see the benefit of the pain you are now experiencing regarding your abortion, but God is trying to work in you—let Him!

How Are You Feeling?*

Emotions—we all have them. Emotions are complex and play an immense role in our lives, for the way we feel about any given

*Grateful acknowledgment is given to Mrs. Jackie Katz for information received from a seminar she conducted for the Wives' Fellowship of Capital Bible Seminary in winter, 1983.

situation influences our thoughts; our thoughts in turn influence our attitudes; and our attitudes affect our dealings with ourselves, other people, and God.

Be glad God has given you emotions! He never wants to take them from you, yet at the same time God desires that you will yield your emotions to His use. Our feelings are indicators to let us know how we are doing in a given area, but they are not to be our guide as to the action we will take. Feelings vary from individual to individual because God created each of us uniquely.

You are responding to your abortion differently than I did to mine. You may experience only one or two adverse feelings, while another woman may be troubled by tremendous emotional upheaval in several areas. Likewise, your individual reaction to anger or grief, for example, will differ from that of any other woman. One woman may "let it all hang out," yet another woman may suffer silently without a word to anyone.

However, our feelings alone do not indicate God's will for us. Since God gave us emotions, we know they have a place in our lives. But we should not rely solely on them for our spiritual guidance. God intends our emotions to be accountable to our reason and will. The philosophy "if it feels good (or right), do it" is not God's philosophy. The Bible admonishes us to test our feelings against what God says: "But examine everything carefully; hold fast to that which is good" (1 Thes. 5:21; see also 1 John 4:1).

Emotions in themselves are neither good nor bad. It is what we *do* with our emotions that determines whether they are sinful. We can choose to do something in spite of the way we feel. If we do what God says in spite of our feelings, we show we love God. Obeying is an expression of our love for God (John 14:15). In order to obey God, we must know what He says regarding our feelings.

While it is important not to deny your feelings regarding your abortion, it is equally important not to let feelings such as grief, anger, or bitterness control your thoughts and actions. Ask yourself, *How do I really feel?* and *Why do I feel this way?* Think through your feelings and determine what you will do with them. If we seek after the flesh (earthly benefits), we will set our minds toward those things that satisfy us at the moment, but if we are yielding ourselves to the power of the Holy Spirit, we will set our minds toward the things that please God (Rom. 8:5).

Christ had to deal with feelings of frustration, fear, and sorrow. How did Christ deal with His feelings? First, He admitted them, then He requested the support of friends. Knowing that emotional suffering could never separate Him from God and that blessing would follow obedience, Christ acted according to God's principles in spite of His negative feelings (Matt. 26:36-39; Heb. 5:7-8). Christ set an excellent example for us.

Our intellect (mind) evaluates what we feel. But it is our will that chooses to obey. As in salvation, so in daily living, God permits us to choose whether to follow Him. Once we know the right way, we must obey whether we "feel" like it or not. "To one who knows the right thing to do, and does not do it, to him it is sin" (James 4:17).

As we look at the negative emotional reactions to abortion, critically examine yourself and honestly admit the areas which are troubling you. You may find you are having difficulty in several of the areas discussed. Work on one problem at a time, trusting the Lord to change you as you set your mind to please Him.

Some Practical Pointers

As we progress through this chapter and the chapters following, I encourage you to look up Scripture passages as they are presented. Discover for yourself what God says in His Word. You will also find a concordance beneficial. A concordance is a listing of words used in the Bible (e.g., anger, love, grief) and the Bible passages in which those words are found. Many Bibles have a partial concordance, but a complete concordance will serve you well as you look up Bible references to find out what God says about a particular emotion.

Another good idea is to make a list of areas in which you have trouble. Divide a piece of paper into four columns. In the first column, carefully list specific actions that you know are not pleasing to God (e.g., losing your temper and throwing something). List only *your* actions, not those of others. God holds you and only you accountable for your actions (Ezek. 18:20). In the second column, state the emotion causing the sinful action (e.g., anger) and related Scriptures that have convicted you of that sin in your life. In the third column, indicate the action or attitude which would please God in the specific instance (e.g., remaining calm) and Scriptures relating to the correct action. In the final column, list specific actions you can do to keep you from committing the sin again (e.g., sit down and think about why you are angry before you respond to the situation).

As you find Bible passages that deal with your specific emotional conflicts, study them, memorize them, and ask God to change your thinking to conform to His Word (Ps. 139:23-24). Then do what God says to do (James 4:17). These Bible verses used in conjunction with suggestions for dealing with each particular emotion should start you on your way to living a joyful and peace-filled life before God, other people, and with yourself.

Others Are Hurting Too

The emotions discussed here are not the only ones indicated on the questionnaires returned to me, but they are the ones most often mentioned as problem areas. For your information (and so you realize that you are *not* alone in your feelings) the breakdown of the forty-six completed questionnaires I received is shown in the accompanying chart.

EMOTION	PRIOR TO ABORTION		AFTER ABORTION	
	Number	Percentage	Number	Percentage
guilt	17	37%	40	87%
grief	—	—	36	78
depression	20	43	35	76
remorse	6	13	35	76
repentance	—	—	34	74
anger	10	22	31	67
shame	19	41	30	65
bitterness	11	24	26	57
fear	39	85	25	54*
frustration	18	39	22	48
anxiety	32	70	23	50*
blameshifting	9	20	19	41
hope	5	11	17	37
self-pity	9	20	17	37
resentfulness	7	15	17	37
doubt	17	37	17	37
peace	2	4	17	37
freedom	—	—	13	28
indignation	3	7	11	24
righteousness	1	—	6	13

*decreased following abortion

Good Grief

Are you grieving? Grief is a deep sense of suffering and is normal following earthshaking occurrences such as death. Usually people mourn the death of someone whom they knew and loved, who is now missed as emptiness rushes in to fill the vacated place.

For those of us who have aborted, grieving does not have the consolation of fond memories. We grieve for a person whose fragile life ended only weeks after it had begun—someone we never knew and realized too late we loved. Your grief may be intensified because of your involvement with your baby's death. However, your own actions in ending your baby's life do not lessen your need to grieve over his death. You may find that remorse, a deep sense of guilt or regret, accompanies your grief.

Your grief caught you by surprise. You didn't expect to have such terrible sorrow following your abortion. At the time you aborted, you may not have realized your actions resulted in the death of another person. Now the fact that a baby—your own child—is dead by your consent may overwhelm you.

Grief is your personal response to the realization that someone is gone, never to be seen again on this earth. Grieving is good unless it leads to despair. But God's Word tells us, "If we have hoped in Christ in this life only, we are of all men most to be pitied" (1 Cor. 15:19). There is a life coming where there will be no sorrow, no tears, only abundant joy (Rev. 21:4). So grieve, but don't despair, for death is not the end in God's eyes.

People express their grief in different ways. Jesus wept at the tomb of His friend Lazarus (John 11:35). Surely if our Lord could weep, so can we. And we know that Jesus wept openly, for in the following verse we read that bystanders remarked, "Behold how He loved him!" (v. 36) Grief shows our love for the dead person.

Sometimes people find themselves unable to grieve by crying. There are other ways to express your grief. (Refer to Jeffrey Watson's book, *Looking Beyond*, also published by Victor Books.) In 2 Chronicles 35:25 we read that Jeremiah mourned Josiah through songs he had composed. It is recorded that David grieved on several occasions. Second Samuel 1:17–27 records the laments David sang over the death of King Saul and his son Jonathan, who was David's closest friend. In 2 Samuel 3:32 David wept at Abner's tomb and then lamented Abner's death by song (vv. 33–34). In this particular instance David's action proved to the people he had no part in Abner's death (v. 37).

In contrast, in 2 Samuel 18:33 David mourned the death of his beloved son Absalom, who died as a consequence of David's sin of adultery with Bathsheba (see 2 Sam. 12:9-12; 18:5, 15). Here David mourned though he was directly responsible for the death of his son. David's grief was so great that he wished he had died instead of Absalom. David's grief affected him so intensely that those around him suffered from his neglect of their needs (2 Sam. 19:1-6). We must take care that in our grief we do not neglect our responsibilities to those around us. In our grief we may not think it possible, but life goes on around us, often oblivious to our grief. Our responsibility is to meet the needs of others during the course of our grieving (2 Sam. 19:7).

The example of Absalom's death because of David and Bathsheba's sin, shows that though God forgives all sin, we may still face the inevitable consequences of our sin. If you have trusted Christ as your Saviour, your part in the death of your unborn child has been forgiven totally and completely (Heb. 10:17), but that does not negate your need to grieve nor natural consequences which may follow (e.g., sadly, you may find yourself unable to bear more children because of complications resulting from your abortion).

You must express your grief outwardly. Cry, mourn in song, write a poem, or keep a diary. Attempts to keep your grief bottled up inside of you will eventually result in depression or other sinful responses to your genuine suffering. Tell God how you feel. Pour out your heart to Him and then listen to His answer as He speaks to you through His Word. God promises comfort: "Blessed are those who mourn, for they shall be comforted" (Matt. 5:4). Those are Christ's own words to you. He will heal your broken heart (Ps. 147:3).

God's love for you is boundless! But don't be surprised if others laugh or ridicule you for mourning your aborted baby. Even people who encouraged you to abort may now take the attitude "you made your bed, now lie in it." But look what Jesus says: "You will be sorrowful, but your sorrow will be turned to joy" (John 16:20). Don't let other people rob you of your real need to grieve, but at the same time realize your grief will pass. Don't try to hang on to it—release it and let it go.

As you grieve, recognize God's sovereignty in your abortion. Nothing happens that God does not permit. This is difficult to understand sometimes, but remember that "*all* things work together for good" (Rom. 8:28, KJV). This includes things that happened in your past and which now affect your future as a child of God.

It is possible that God used your abortion to bring you to salvation or to bring you back into a closer relationship with Himself. Perhaps your grief was not so much for your child as it was over the wrong you had done. Second Corinthians 7:8-11 speaks to this. The Apostle Paul had written a letter admonishing the Corinthians to get the sin out of their lives. This made the Corinthians sad, yet Paul wrote: "I now rejoice, not that you were made sorrowful, but that you were made sorrowful to the point of repentance" (v. 9).

Here we see the difference between an apology and a confession. When you apologize, you say "I'm sorry you caught me," but when you confess, you say "I'm sorry I did it." And repentance means you turn away from your sin and do right from that point on. If you mourned your sin of abortion to the point of repentance, your abortion, though a terrible experience for you to live with, was not in vain. God allowed it and now you must trust Him to see you through your grief and pain.

Christ never condemned those who grieved. Instead, He offered comfort. And indeed we have a Comforter today whom Christ left in His place when He returned to heaven. "I will pray the Father, and He shall give you another Comforter, that He may abide with you forever" (John 14:16, KJV). The Holy Spirit is that comforter and lives within each believer today.

As you express your grief, you will discover that releasing your sorrow will help cleanse you from the terrible hurt of your loss. However, be aware that grief tends to expose guilt, fear, and anger over the situation in which you find yourself. These emotional responses to your grief must be dealt with biblically. As you work through your emotional conflicts, your grief will begin to pass as you respond to your feelings and thoughts in a way pleasing to God. Remember to thank God for working in your life (1 Thes. 5:18).

Finally, seek opportunities to comfort others who grieve. Perhaps your parents or husband share your grief over your abortion. They lost a child also. Go to them, cry with them, comfort them. In giving of yourself in this way, you will find you too are comforted. "[God] comforteth us in all our tribulation, that we may be able to comfort them which are in any trouble, by the comfort wherewith we ourselves are comforted" (2 Cor. 1:4, KJV).

Who's to Blame?
Well-meaning advice often tells a person not to be too hard on herself. You may have been told that since you were influenced by others, since the law legalized abortion, since you were so afraid, or since your circumstances warranted an abortion, that you were not totally to blame for your abortion. Blaming others for our actions is not new. In the Garden of Eden, Adam blamed Eve and Eve in turn blamed the serpent when confronted by God after disobeying His command not to eat of the forbidden fruit (Gen. 3:12-13). Blameshifting is an old and often used excuse.

In seeking someone to blame for our abortions, I wonder how many of us have blamed God for allowing it to happen? After all, we reason, God *could* have stopped it. "A man's own folly ruins his life, yet his heart rages against the Lord" (Prov. 19:3, NIV).

Following my abortion, I found it easy to cast blame onto my mother, the doctor who actually performed my abortion, and God. Perhaps you too have your own list of people you blame. While it may be true that other people are also guilty concerning your abortion, that does not negate your own guilt in the act.

You are responsible for your own actions. We are never forced to sin by what someone has done to us. You and I are victims of our own selfish actions. As we saw previously, whether we aborted to please someone else or purely for personal gain, every abortion is ultimately done for selfish reasons. We must face that fact. Regardless of our situation, we could have said, "No, I won't abort." The abortion was done at our consent. We thought we saw an easy way out and now that guilt has reared its ugly head, we seek to find another means of escape by blaming someone else.

The only one who has the right to cast blame is God, yet He refuses to do so if you are a Christian. "There is therefore now no condemnation for those who are in Christ Jesus" (Rom. 8:1). Those are wonderful words to hear. You were to blame and now God no longer condemns you. Why continue to shift the blame to others? They carry their own load of guilt and would benefit most from your sharing Christ with them.

Good-bye to Guilt

Salvation canceled all your sins through the death of Christ. You may have trusted Christ as Saviour, and yet you still *feel* guilty. My hurting friend, once Christ is your personal Saviour, the guilt you feel is no longer yours to bear. It is now not sin that makes you feel guilty, but rather your feeling guilty has become sin. You are not trusting that God did what He said He would do—cleanse you from *all* sin. Your sin of abortion was atoned for on your behalf—you are no longer guilty.

In ancient times when a person was cast into prison, a list of his or her debts was recorded. When the debts were satisfied, the words *It is finished* were written across the list of debts. Now think of Christ as the One upon whom all your debts (sins) were written. Your debts were nailed to the cross in the form of Jesus Christ. When Christ, in His final words, cried out "It is finished," He was canceling your debt by paying the price for you (John 19:30). If you have trusted Christ as your personal Saviour, you now possess a receipt marked "It is finished." It's your proof that the reason for your guilt is gone. The debt has been paid.

Each time you permit yourself to feel guilty about your abortion, it is as if you were running to the cross to pound one more nail into Christ's body. You are saying to God, "I don't believe this one debt is paid." You are not trusting Christ's death as sufficient for paying *all* your sin—as though it were too big for Him to handle alone. If you belong to Christ, the debt *is* paid, and the reason for your guilt is gone.

You are free from guilt regarding your abortion. Thank God for this assurance and claim it as your own. "If therefore the Son shall make you free, you shall be free indeed" (John 8:36). The weight of the sin of your abortion is gone! Praise God for the freedom from guilt you now enjoy in Christ. Thank God for His forgiveness regarding your abortion. "How blessed is he whose transgression is forgiven, whose sin is covered! How blessed is the man to whom the Lord does not impute iniquity, and in whose spirit there is no deceit" (Ps. 32:1-2). Rejoice, for your sins are covered by the blood of Christ—completely, totally, eternally.

God has forgiven you, but there is another aspect of forgiveness that is often overlooked. This aspect of forgiveness involves extending to others what Christ has given you. "For if you forgive men for their transgressions, your Heavenly Father will also forgive you. But if you do not forgive men, then your Father will not forgive your transgression" (Matt. 6:14-15). Our forgiveness of others affects our fellowship with them and with God, but not our salvation.

Matthew 18:21-35 is the Parable of the Unforgiving Servant. The parable begins with Peter asking Christ how many times one person should forgive another person. Christ tells Peter to forgive 490 times! In other words, forgive as long as necessary. Christ then says:

> For this reason the kingdom of heaven may be compared to a certain king who wished to settle accounts with his slaves. And when he had begun to settle them, there was brought to him one who owed him ten thousand talents. But since he did not have the means to repay, his lord commanded him to be sold, along with his wife and children and all that he had, and repayment to be made.
>
> The slave therefore falling down, prostrated himself before him, saying, "Have patience with me, and I will repay you everything." And the lord of that slave felt compassion and released him and forgave him the debt.
>
> But that slave went out and found one of his fellow slaves who owed him a hundred denarii; and he seized him and began to choke him, saying, "Pay back what you owe."
>
> So his fellow slave fell down and began to entreat him, saying, "Have patience with me and I will repay you."
>
> He was unwilling however, but went and threw him in prison until he should pay back what was owed. So when his fellow slaves saw what had happened, they were deeply grieved and came and reported to their lord all that had happened.
>
> Then summoning him, his lord said to him, "You wicked slave, I forgave you all that debt because you entreated me. Should you not also have had mercy on your fellow slave, even as I had mercy on you?" And his lord, moved with anger, handed him over to the torturers until he should repay all that was owed him.
>
> So shall My Heavenly Father also do to you, if each of

you does not forgive his brother from your heart (Matt. 18:23–35).

God has graciously forgiven you all your sins. Don't permit yourself to be so cold as not to forgive the sins others have committed against you. Is there someone you need to forgive? The doctors and nurses who performed your abortion? The counseling service that encouraged you to abort? What about your parents or boyfriend who pressured you? What about those who may be laughing at you even now for your newfound faith in God? Christ says forgive. He does not say forgive if you *feel* like it or forgive for certain circumstances. He says *forgive*. And He has given us an example.

Christ, as He was being tried prior to His crucifixion, did not open His mouth in His own defense (Isa. 53:7). Instead, He silently took the blame for our sins. Then, as He hung upon the cross in His final moments before death, He prayed, "Father, forgive them; for they do not know what they are doing" (Luke 23:34).

Those who "helped" you to abort did not realize what they were doing either, just as you didn't. Forgive them before God, and if the opportunity presents itself, tell them you forgive them for what they did.

If you have wronged people by verbally accusing them of participating in your abortion, or have hurt them by your actions because of their role, you have some repairing to do. Go to those people and tell them you are sorry for your improper attitude and actions toward them (Matt. 5:23-24). Ask for their forgiveness. Then do not bring the matter up again for discussion. Consider it over and done with. Don't be troubled if the person does not forgive you. As you know, people tend to harbor ill feelings. Once you have done what God requires of *you*, your conscience is cleansed from guilt.

Do you still feel guilty? Is there unconfessed sin in your life? Is there someone you need to forgive or from whom you need to seek forgiveness? Don't let your pride keep you from removing all your guilt. "He who conceals his transgressions will not prosper, but he who confesses and forsakes them will find compassion" (Prov. 28:13).

Lesson from a Parable

Luke 15:11-32 is the well-known story of the prodigal son. A father had two sons and divided his wealth between them. The younger son took his portion and went off to pursue the "good life." After squandering his fortune, he fed hogs to support himself. "But when he came to his senses," he realized that his father's hired servants lived better than he did. The son determined to go to his father and say, "Father, I have sinned against heaven, and in your sight; I am no longer worthy to be called your son; make me as one of your hired men."

The son set out for home, but when he was still a long way off, his father saw him and had compassion on him and hugged him. The son confessed his sin to his father as he had determined to do. But the father would not hear of his son in any position but as his son and set about preparing a banquet in his honor. The son *accepted* his father's forgiveness.

In this parable we see that the younger son saw his guilt, acknowledged his sin, and sought forgiveness from both God and man. The father in turn forgave the son for his wrong conduct and restored him to his former position. Finally, the son accepted his father's forgiveness. What a beautiful picture of our present relationship with our Heavenly Father! Now put yourself in this picture and whenever Satan attacks your mind with guilt feelings regarding your abortion, say "I am forgiven." Then ask God to give you something good to think about. He will.

But It's So Frustrating!

Hasn't it been a frustrating experience to have endured an abortion only to discover that the peace and freedom the abortion was to bring to your life has eluded you? Frustration, by dictionary definition, is a rendering worthless of efforts directed to some specific end. It means that certain circumstances have prevented you from receiving the gratification you sought. Perhaps you have lost your boyfriend or husband anyway; maybe you want children now and cannot have them; people don't understand; your emotions are in turmoil over an action you are helpless to change. Your actions have not benefited you at all.

You may know other women who have submitted to an abortion, or who are rushing to a clinic in the same frantic flight of panic as you once did. Your frustration grows as you must sit by virtually helpless to assist these women who will one day face the same emotional aftermath you now face.

When I think about frustration, one person stands out in my mind—the Old Testament Prophet Habakkuk. This godly man asked the questions: Why does evil prosper? Why does God look upon the evil in the world with a seemingly indifferent attitude? Why are we permitted to look upon the evil while at the same time are helpless to stop its rush to destruct the innocent? (Hab. 1:2–4) WHY?

Things were not much different in Habakkuk's day than they are now. Dr. Charles L. Feinberg states:

> Miscarriage of justice was the order of the day. Ensnaring the righteous by fraud, the ungodly perverted all right and honesty. Because God did not punish sin immediately, men thought they could sin on with impunity.[1]

And so we too find ourselves asking—why are helpless preborn children slaughtered by the millions every year? Don't You care, Lord? Why do You allow women to be deceived into aborting their children? Why, Lord? Aren't You going to do anything about this situation?

God does not leave Habakkuk, nor us, without an answer. God is indeed intimately involved in the affairs of people (Hab. 1:5). However, part of the reason He permits evil to prosper is in order to chastise His children (believers) who have done wrong. The Book of Habakkuk refers specifically to God's chastisement of the nation Israel (1:6–11). However, we can apply the principles to our lives, for in Hebrews 12:5–11 we see that it is a loving act of God that He should "spank" us for wrongdoing.

> And you have forgotten the exhortation which is addressed to you as sons, "My son, do not regard lightly the discipline of the Lord, nor faint when you are reproved by Him; for those whom the Lord loves He disciplines, and He scourges every son who He receives." It is for discipline that you endure; God deals with you as with sons; for what son is there whom his father does not discipline? But if you are without discipline, of

which all have become partakers, then you are illegitimate children and not sons. Furthermore, we had
earthly fathers to discipline us, and we respected them;
shall we not much rather be subject to the Father of
spirits, and live? For they [our earthly fathers] disci-
plined us for a short time as seemed best to them, but
He [God] disciplines us for our good, that we may share
His holiness. All discipline for the moment seems not to
be joyful, but sorrowful; yet to those who have been
trained by it, afterwards it yields the peaceful fruit of
righteousness.

These verses tell us of God's great love for us and His concern
that we correct our sinful ways. As God chastens us, we are to be
thankful and to learn (Ps. 94:12; Job 5:17-18).

The second reason God gives for permitting the righteous to
suffer is to produce patience in us. Patience is that inner quality
that permits us to wait calmly but expectantly to see what God
will do.

Consider it all joy, my brethren, when you encounter
various trials, knowing that the testing of your faith produces endurance. And let endurance have its perfect
result, that you may be perfect and complete, lacking
nothing (James 1:2-4).

Trials are God's method of developing patience in us in order to
mature us as Christians.

The second half of Habakkuk 2:4 says, "But the righteous will
live by his faith." (See also Rom. 1:17; Gal. 3:11; Heb. 10:38.) We
are to trust God completely, knowing that what He does will be
loving and just (Ps. 37:7-11). We are to live by our faith in God as
the sovereign ruler of the universe. Because God is loving and
just, we have the assurance that the fate of the millions of aborted
children *is* of concern to Him. He cares equally for aborted
women. God *is* working. To our eyes, it may seem those who
perform and advocate abortion get away with murder. But to
God, who keeps accurate records, a day of judgment is coming.

Though we may not like it, there are reasons God allows certain events to occur that He has chosen not to explain to us. We
must trust God to do what is best. That does not mean you must

sit idly by. However, as you attempt to talk a woman out of aborting, for instance, do not become frustrated if she ignores your wise counsel. God is working in her life and she may have to endure the same nightmare as you in order for her to see the helplessness of her sinful condition. You may choose to write to legislators and make your beliefs known regarding abortion. Do not become frustrated if these people choose to go in another direction. Know that God is in control of all our leaders and has placed them in the positions they hold (Rom. 13:1). God will let evil prevail for His determined time and then He will cause those perpetrating evil to fall. Pray for God to act swiftly to change the path our nation is taking, to change the minds of women, to bring us back into a state of sexual morality.

Praise God for His power and His person. Continue to uplift the name of God to others and to declare that God is working, is vitally interested in what is happening, and will see His will done. Then with Habakkuk, you can exclaim: "The Lord God is my strength" (3:19) and I will be patient and trust Him although I do not understand why things are so (Rom. 8:28-31).

Taking the Bite Out of Bitterness

Have you ever bitten unsuspectingly into a piece of unsweetened chocolate? Upon tasting it, your expression changes, your mouth forms an ugly expression, and your teeth grit together as your tongue yearns to escape the acrid taste. You say, "Augh! That's awful!" And though you spit it out, the bitter aftertaste lingers.

Bitterness, that awful taste existing internally, manifests itself in your face and words. The emotion of bitterness is distasteful or distressing to the mind and is usually marked by contempt or complaining. Resentment is akin to bitterness, but is less intense. Bitterness grows out of resentment into hate, with increasing and persistent thoughts of ill-will regarding something or someone who has wronged or insulted or injured you.

God views bitterness as great discontentment—a root of trouble: "See to it that no one comes short of the grace of God; that no root of bitterness springing up causes trouble, and by it many be defiled" (Heb. 12:15). Bitterness defiles us as we give in to its demands—as we permit it to take root in us, to flourish and grow, to spread itself as it creeps and grips each part of our being on its winding path through our minds.

The eight short verses of 2 Samuel 6:16-23 present a picture of a bitter woman, Michal. We know that Michal was King David's wife and originally loved him (1 Sam. 18:20, 28), and helped save David's life from her father Saul's relentless conspiracy (1 Sam. 19:11-17). What caused her change of attitude so that she now "despised him in her heart"? (2 Sam. 6:16) We know that prior to the event described in 2 Samuel 6 David married two other women, Abigail and Ahinoam and that Saul had taken Michal from David and had given her as wife to a man named Palti (1 Sam. 25:43-44).[2] Later we read that David demanded Michal be returned to him (2 Sam. 3:13-14). Palti accompanies Michal to David "weeping as he went," but was sent away (v. 16). From this we may discern that Michal came to resent David for taking her from Palti, a man whom she loved and who obviously loved her. Michal may have also resented David's other wives. We don't know. What we can learn from this is that Michal's great discontent manifested itself in her words and actions on the day of David's great rejoicing. Michal, because of her bitterness, attempted to ruin David's joy. In 2 Samuel 6:23 we read that the only person she hurt was herself, for God kept her barren, which in those days was the greatest shame a woman could incur.

By contrast, let's examine the life of a person who had every reason to become bitter. Genesis 37–50 records the history of Joseph, probably best known to most of us for his coat of many colors. Because he was his father's favorite son, Joseph's jealous brothers sold him into slavery. Eventually Joseph was purchased by Potiphar and came to be appointed the captain of Pharaoh's bodyguards. Potiphar's wife tried to seduce Joseph, but he rejected her advances. Angered, she falsely accused Joseph of rape, whereupon he was cast into prison. There Joseph was asked to interpret the dreams of the chief cupbearer and the baker. Joseph did as asked and in turn requested the cupbearer to tell Pharaoh of his unjust imprisonment, which the cupbearer promised to do. Two years passed and still Joseph remained in prison. Finally, the cupbearer remembered his promise and told Pharaoh of Joseph. Joseph was released.

Joseph had reason to become bitter—betrayed, lied against, and forgotten—but Joseph chose to see God's hand in his life. God honored Joseph's attitude and eventually placed him in the position of prime minister over all Egypt, second only to Pharaoh. During a famine several years later, Joseph had occasion to assist and acknowledge his brothers. With love in his heart, Joseph told his fear-stricken brothers, "And as for you, you meant evil against me, but God meant it for good in order to bring about this present result, to preserve many people alive" (Gen. 50:20).

Joseph concentrated on doing his best for God as he served his masters faithfully, helped those he could, and literally waited patiently for God to work.

Bitterness is sin and God commands us to put off bitterness: "Let all bitterness and wrath and anger and clamor and slander be put away from you, along with all malice" (Eph. 4:31). Putting off the incorrect responses to your abortion is not enough, however. You must replace the old emotions with truth, love, and forgiveness (Eph. 4:32).

God wants to remove *your* bitterness, if only you will let Him. But we often become so hard, so cold, and so indifferent that we fail to see our bitterness as sin. Before you can rid yourself of this emotion, you must admit it is sin—then God can begin to work in your life.

First Corinthians 13 reveals God's antidote to bitterness.

> Love is patient, love is kind, and is not jealous; love does not brag and is not arrogant, does not act unbecomingly; it does not seek its own, is not provoked, does not take into account a wrong suffered, does not rejoice in unrighteousness, but rejoices with the truth; bears all things, believes all things, hopes all things, endures all things. Love never fails (1 Cor. 13:4-8).

The love referred to in this passage is *agape* in the Greek. This is the same love Christ had for you when He took your place on the cross. An unconditional love, it is offered without thought of gain or reward. It is love that loves even when the person loved hates you in return. It is God's love manifested in you toward others.

As you put off bitterness, you must put on love. Think of bitterness as a filthy, torn, old garment that you put off, casting it away from your body. Now think of love as a freshly laundered garment you put on to replace the old, useless garment. It is vital to understand that putting on love is an act of the will (Col. 3:14-15; see also John 13:34-35). You *can* love whether or not you feel like it. Not only is love an act of the will, love is also learned. Practicing loving thoughts and actions will result in changed feelings. I realize that loving and praying for the people who urged you to abort may be difficult at first. Pray for them anyway. Ask God to remove your bitterness and replace it with love for the people in spite of their sins (Prov. 10:12). Begin to correct relationships with those intimately involved with your abortion (Prov. 3:27; 25:21-22). Refuse to allow your mind to dwell on people who had nothing to do with your abortion, but who now appear to torment your mind. For example, when you see a pregnant woman or a woman with a baby, do not feel bitterness toward her because she has something you thought you did not want. She had nothing to do with your abortion. Instead, rejoice for that woman and for the new life God has given her.

Alleviating Anger

I was misinformed! I was pressured! I was deceived! I was lied to! Irritated, I keep my mind focused on the object of my distress . . . desire for revenge begins to grow . . . then POW! I lash out in a rage at anyone, anything. I stamp my feet. I scream and shout as a turbulent torrent of malicious words tumbles from my snarled lips. Perhaps I even go so far as to physically strike out at my husband or children. I throw a plate and it meets the floor in a thousand tiny splinters. Ahhhh! Momentarily I feel better—all that fury within me has been released.

You have just read the traditional description of anger, but anger can take another avenue quite the opposite from the above description. As I move from irritation to anger, I can choose to restrain myself and keep my anger inside. There it festers until a deep-seated bitterness continually eats away at me. I dwell on thoughts of evil toward those who have hurt me. Because I have clammed up, ulcers may develop. In an effort to control my emotions, I pretend not to be angry. I don't feel better, but my problems are my own, and for the most part, except for an occasional lapse when a complaint or contemptuous word escapes, no one realizes just how angry I am.

Anger—that emotional reaction we utilize when we fail to get our own way—results from selfishness. The capacity for anger lies within each of us. Anger is unpredictable and can't be hidden, but it can be controlled. Did you know that? For instance, you are in a heated argument with your husband or boyfriend. The phone rings. You pick up the receiver and in your sweetest, calmest voice say "hello." You continue your conversation to its conclusion, then hang up. Interrupted in the midst of an anger attack, you have just controlled your outburst.

Anger desires to punish someone or something for wrongs done to us. When we internalize anger, it becomes bitterness, most often exhibited by brooding or animosity as we complain and look upon the object of our anger with contempt.

Wrath, on the other hand, is the external display of anger and exhibits a strong desire for revenge or an antagonistic hostility toward the one who precipitated our anger. It strikes out visibly in an effort to appease itself.

Man views anger as a means to release destructive emotions or as something to be controlled and kept chained inside of you. As we explore what God says regarding anger, we will discover both of these "solutions" are wrong. Not only are they wrong, but they will not work on a permanent basis.

Anger is not sinful when it is justified and controlled. Mark Porter states in his article, "Just How Righteous Is Our Anger?": "Perhaps we should define righteous indignation as anger aroused by the unjust treatment of *others*"[3] (italics added). I think that's a good definition and is what Jesus taught by example. He became angered with the Pharisees over their legalistic lack of concern for people (Mark 3:1-5).

Anger does not have to be explosive to be sinful. Last week I spoke with a man who quietly and calmly told me he prayed that the justices on the Supreme Court who were pro-abortion would die. His anger at the injustice the Justices condoned led this man to sin. God doesn't want us to seek revenge for the wrongs others do. "Never take your own revenge, beloved, but leave room for the wrath of God, for it is written, 'Vengeance is Mine, I will repay,' says the Lord" (Rom. 12:19).

Proverbs 29:11 tells us a wise person refrains from letting his or her anger control her. We know that Jesus was angry when He saw the money changers desecrating the temple (Matt. 21:12-13), but He dealt with the situation in a decisive but sinless manner (Heb. 4:15).

Anger is sinful when it comes from wrong motives such as jealousy, suspicion, or resentment. It is wrong when it results from you not getting your own way or when you react too quickly without investigating the facts. Anger is wrong when it causes destruction to a person or situation (Eph. 4:29; Matt. 5:22), as in Peter's case when he cut off Malchus' ear (John 18:10-

11). Your response must always be in conformity to God's Word. In Romans 12:14-21 we find that God tells us to bless those who persecute us (v. 14); never to repay evil with evil (v. 17); to be at peace with all men (v. 18); and to never take our own revenge (v. 19). Instead, we are to lovingly care for our enemy (v. 20).

If you have been sinfully angry—that is if your anger has lingered, is selfish, or attacks someone verbally or physically, you need to acknowledge your sin to God. Tell God you realize that your angry thoughts are sin in His eyes. Tell Him you are sorry and ask Him to help you to overcome your anger. Now ask God to teach you to be "quick to hear, slow to speak, and slow to anger; for the anger of man does not achieve the righteousness of God" (James 1:19-20).

When others talk about abortion and your anger begins to build, resist the impulse to spout out your verbal vengeance. Do not participate in activities that may intensify your anger. Picketing abortion clinics in a peaceful way is legal and may help make people aware of the atrocity of abortion. However, if your tendency is to let anger govern your words and actions, you may find yourself going beyond expressing your disapproval to revenging yourself by inappropriate action. Remember, when you are doing God's will, you will be at peace with yourself in any given situation.

Getting rid of your anger is not enough. The sinful response must always be replaced with a godly one. In conquering your anger, remember that with God's help you can control your emotions whether you feel like it or not. In order to be angry and sin not, your anger must be without hatred or resentment; it must be controlled and directed at something evil or wrong. Your anger may be justified, but the way you express it may be wrong.

Dr. Jay Adams says that the secret to resolving your anger is to release it under control.[4] Do not hold it inside—release it. Do not release it in a fury—control it. If necessary and justified, confront the person in a proper way (Eph. 4:15). Don't incite others to anger (Prov. 20:2). Finally, deal with your anger before you end each day (Eph. 4:26). If possible, tell the person who wronged you what he has done. And remember, you are not accountable for *his* response!

If you were pressured by someone else to abort, forgive that person before God (Col. 3:13; Eph. 4:32). Realize that though they were wrong, your anger will now only harm you. Memorize

Ephesians 4:32 and meditate upon it, especially when you are tempted with angry thoughts. God didn't have to send Christ to die. He did it because He loves you. Porter comments: "When we begin to grasp how much God has forgiven us, it becomes easier for us to forgive others. Forgiveness means overlooking an offense."[5] We need to love those who used us, who lied to us. We don't *have* to forgive and love them, but if we don't, our lives will be miserable because we have refused to obey God.

Pray for the doctors and nurses who performed your abortion. Ask God to give them no rest until they repent of their sins. Be angry at the sin, not at the sinner.

Proverbs has several passages dealing with anger. They tell what results when anger is sinfully displayed and also the value of self-control in anger situations:

> A quick-tempered man acts foolishly, and a man of evil devices is hated (Prov. 14:17).

> He who is slow to anger has great understanding, but he who is quick-tempered exalts folly (14:29).

> A gentle answer turns away wrath, but a harsh word stirs up anger (15:1).

> A hot-tempered man stirs up strife, but the slow to anger pacifies contention (15:18).

> He who is slow to anger is better than the mighty, and he who rules his spirit, than he who captures a city (16:32).

> A man's discretion makes him slow to anger, and it is his glory to overlook a transgression (19:11).

> Do not associate with a man given to anger; or go with a hot-tempered man, lest you learn his ways, and find a snare for yourself (22:24-25).

> The north wind brings forth rain, and a backbiting tongue an angry countenance (25:23).

> Like charcoal to hot embers and wood to fire, so is a contentious man to kindle strife (26:21).

An angry man stirs up strife, and a hot-tempered man abounds in transgression (29:22).

Anger hurts you and others. With God's help, you *can* eliminate sinful anger from your life.

Dealing with Depression

Let's begin by defining depression. It is more than discouragement, more than disappointment, more than being "down," and more than "feeling blue." Depression goes beyond despair to find its depths in feelings of worthlessness and hopelessness and is sometimes accompanied by suicidal thoughts or attempts. Jonah 4:3 describes the mindset of a depressed person: "Therefore now, O Lord, please take my life from me, for death is better to me than life."

Though most of us probably do not suffer from true depression, we often experience "down" days. The term *depression* used in this section refers to feeling "blue" or "down."

Depression can be attributed to two causes: physical and mental. Depression caused by physical reasons comes upon its victim unwelcomed and unbidden. A particular illness may be accompanied by depression or it may originate from taking any one of a number of drugs. Because of illness you may be taking medication that causes depression.

The other type of depression is mental and stems from self-pity. It is perhaps the most common and most misunderstood form of depression. It can affect your body physically with genuine illness if given enough time and can be intensified by taking drugs, either legal or nonlegal. Depression caused by self-pity can be overcome, but you are the only person who can determine its termination. It is this mental depression that the aborted woman must deal with if she is to have victory and complete release from her tormented mind.

Depression is not new to me. I lived in a depressed state of mind off and on for years due to emotional reactions within myself regarding my abortion.

For we who have endured one or more abortions, depression can be caused by dwelling on our due date each year or focusing on the anniversary of our abortion; realization of our failure to face responsibility and carry our baby to term; or dwelling on details of our abortion experience. Underlying all these causes for depression is guilt—guilt that comes from a failure to handle our problems God's way.

You must not permit yourself to dwell on the child you have lost. The Bible instructs us to think on those things which are right, pure, and lovely (Phil. 4:8). Anyone who dwells on the loss of a loved one would soon find themselves depressed. Thinking of how much they miss that person, or of what they wish they had done for them while they lived deepens the sense of guilt. For those of us who have aborted, we can only reflect on what it *could* have been like had our child been born. We can only think from the perspective of how we *might* have intertwined our life with his. Focusing on this only leads to depression.

Instead, we need to get our eyes off ourselves and on God and others. Then we must *do* what is right. Did you know that our feelings don't have to affect our behavior, but our behavior always affects our feelings? For instance, you had an abortion. The emotion of guilt leaps forth. If you spend your days dwelling on that guilt and acting guilty, you will soon find your emotion of guilt deepened and intensified.

Bob George, in his article "There's No Need to Be Depressed," says:

> Depression is not something you catch like a cold. It's something you bring upon yourself by free choice. . . . The battle is won in our minds.[6]

King David, the person God refers to as "a man after God's own heart," struggled with depression.

> For my iniquities are gone over my head; as a heavy burden they weigh too much for me. My wounds grow foul and fester. Because of my folly, I am bent over and greatly bowed down; I go mourning all day long. For my loins are filled with burning; and there is no soundness in my flesh. I am benumbed and badly crushed; I groan because of the agitation of my heart (Ps. 38:4-8).

David's sin even afflicted him physically and mentally:

> When I kept silent about my sin, my body wasted away through my groaning all day long. For day and night

Thy hand was heavy upon me; my vitality was drained away as with the fever heat of summer (Ps. 32:3-4).

Verse 5 reveals the remedy for depression:

I acknowledged my sin to Thee, and my iniquity I did not hide; I said, "I will confess my transgressions to the Lord"; and Thou didst forgive the guilt of my sin.

In Psalm 51 David confessed his sin and asked for forgiveness and restoration to a healthy mind. Psalm 13 describes a person depressed from the sin of self-pity and his recovery as he turns to God for cleansing.

How do we conquer depression? First, we admit it is sin caused by sinful emotional responses which we have permitted to control our thoughts (1 John 1:8-9). Second, we renew our minds, setting our thoughts on God (Rom. 12:1-2). Things may be bad, but we have God's promises that they are not hopeless. Because God has already lovingly forgiven you your past sins, you can thank God as you claim Romans 15:13 for yourself:

Now may the God of hope fill you with all joy and peace in believing, that you may abound in hope by the power of the Holy Spirit.

Now that you have taken your eyes off yourself, you must focus them on someone else. Philippians 2:3-4 offers God's wise counsel:

Do nothing from selfishness or empty conceit, but with humility of mind let each of you regard one another as more important than himself; do not merely look out for your own personal interests, but also for the interests of others.

You see, when you are thinking on the needs and value of others, you won't have time to become depressed! Sure, there are still going to be "down" days, but be careful to fill those days by *doing* what God says even though you don't "feel" like it (Gal. 5:17; Matt. 26:41). Dr. Jay Adams states:

The key to warding off depression, then, is this: do not follow your feelings when you know that you have a responsibility to discharge. Instead, against your feelings, you must do as you should. And when you do, even if at first you do so mechanically, simply because you want to please God and you know that He wants you to do this, in time your feelings will change. God will give you a sense of satisfaction and accomplishment and at length enthusiasm for what you dreaded previously. You must not wait until you feel like it, or you may never feel like doing that task. Nor must you try to change your feelings directly; you cannot do that. Do what you know God wants you to do, WHETHER YOU FEEL LIKE IT OR NOT, and a change in feelings will take place, as a by-product, in time. That is the secret of turning back the tide of depression once it begins to overwhelm you. There is no other way.[7]

A question now remains: Do you really *want* to resolve your depression, or are you content wallowing in self-pity?

A Root Problem
Though the topic discussed in this section is not an emotion, I include it here because it results from incorrect responses to emotions and at the same time causes sinful emotional responses with regard to abortion.

A woman wrote that she "hated her boyfriend for getting her pregnant." Another woman, who has had several abortions, says, "I kill their babies for them and they don't care about me." Both of these women are blameshifting. Both are bitterly angry, frustrated, and most probably depressed. However, at the base of all these problems lies the truth that both of these women are guilty of a sin they have refused to admit.

The root of the abortion problem for most of us goes back prior to our abortions to the fact that our babies were conceived in a sinful relationship. If we had been the chaste women God commands us to be, the "need" for an abortion would never have arisen. Could it be that you are still maintaining a relationship with a man that is sinful? It may not "feel" like sin, you may not really care that it is sin (Prov. 30:20), but until the sin is confessed, repented of, and forgiven, you cannot deal with your other problems (Prov. 28:13).

If you are having sexual relations with anyone other than your husband, God says you are sinning and are in danger of His judgment (Heb. 13:4). Regardless of this, many women have expressed the need to be wanted, loved, or secure as valid reasons for committing adultery or fornication. These women equate sex with acceptance. To many others, sex is a way to prove to themselves and to others that they are independent, their "own boss." Seeking to be somebody or seeking security in immoral relationships is contrary to God's plan for you. God says when you are in Christ (are a Christian), you already *are* somebody very special (Gal. 4:7) and your security is guaranteed (Heb. 13:5).

If you are a Christian and are committing adultery, you are probably experiencing a very real sense of fear. You know your actions are wrong (Ps. 90:8). Guilt causes genuine fear. You have a reason to be afraid until you correct your sinful conduct. There is no gentle way to ease you out of the sin of immorality. God is instructing you in the choice you should make (Ps. 25:12). The only way to deal with fornication is to end the relationship immediately and permanently.

It will not be easy in most instances. You may have formed a deep emotional attachment to your boyfriend. Walking away from him—for good—will hurt you and him. But God promises never to leave you or forsake you—that means He will see you through the emotional upheaval you face, just as He will see you through your abortion aftermath. From personal experience, I can tell you that without the Lord's help, you can never break the cycle of immorality. A sin once committed is easier to commit the second time, and so on, until your actions don't seem so very bad at all. In fact, you come to view immoral sex as proper and good, if not with the father of your aborted baby, then with someone else. And if you should become pregnant again, considering an abortion may slip easily into your mind as you rationalize that it really wasn't so bad after all. Sin always leads to more sin.

God's Word tells you to flee fornication because when you have immoral sex you sin against your own body which is where the Holy Spirit dwells if you are a Christian (1 Cor. 6:18-19). But God also tells you that He has turned you over to your own desires because you have refused to love and to obey Him (Rom. 1:21-22, 24, 28-32).

Thank God we can be free from the sin that once held us in

bondage. Admit your sexual sin (1 John 1:8), confess it (1 John 1:9), claim Philippians 4:13 as your strength, and walk away from that immoral relationship a truly free woman (John 8:10-11).

What to Do for a Change

God has given us clear methods of properly dealing with our emotions. The problem is that you may find the instructions difficult to follow. Do you really *want* to resolve your conflicts regarding your abortion? With God's help you can, but it will mean some changes in the way you think, react, and act regarding your abortion. You know the way you have been dealing with your abortion has not worked. God has the answer to *any* problem you face, but you must *change* in order to apply the solution to your life.

The following six steps are essential for this change:

1. Recognize your areas of sin (1 John 1:8).

2. Repent of your sin (1 John 1:9).

3. Request God's help in dependence upon Him (1 John 5:14-15).

4. Relinquish your sinful thoughts or actions (Rom. 6:5-7; Col. 3:8-9).

5. Replace your sinful thoughts or actions with a godly response (Col. 3:10; Rom. 12:1-2).

6. Repeat, until your godly response becomes a habit (John 3:21; Col. 3:23).

Let me remind you that before you take these six steps, you must first accept Christ's atonement on your behalf. Until you come by faith to receive Christ as your personal Saviour, all attempts to overcome your abortion aftermath are done in your own strength. You must resolve your conflicts through God's power and this can only be accomplished if you are His child.

I fully realize the ways presented in this chapter are contrary to the way the world would have you deal with your abortion aftermath. Without the Holy Spirit to guide you, the solutions presented in this chapter would appear foolish (1 Cor. 1:18-21), and you would not understand why they will work. But they *will* work, and as you begin to practice God's solutions, you will begin to see the fruit of the Holy Spirit in your life.

Galatians 5:19-21 contains a list of things that God hates. Included are immorality, impurity, enmities, strife, jealousy, outbursts of anger, disputes, and envying. These are the things we desire to remove from our lives. We practiced these in the past, but do not wish to continue in this sinful way.

As you begin to deal with your sinful emotional responses to your abortion in a way pleasing to God, you will find that the Holy Spirit will begin to produce fruit in your life. Galatians 5:22-23 lists nine parts to the fruit of the Holy Spirit: love, joy, peace, patience, kindness, goodness, faithfulness, gentleness, and self-control. These are the results of proper responses to emotions that once overwhelmed you to the point of despair. Look for them in your life as you begin to solve your problems God's way.

Some things God asks will be difficult for you to do. Remember 1 Corinthians 10:13. Christians may never say "I can't" to God's instructions. The words *I can* in Philippians 4:13 are followed by "do all things *through Christ.*" That's the secret—Christ stands beside you to help, to guide, to strengthen. Draw on His power.

Realize that your natural tendency will be to return to your negative thought patterns. You may be encouraged to go your own way by other people who may ridicule you as you apply biblical principles to your life. Expect it, but don't allow ungodly attitudes and advice to keep you from having victory over your problems. Understand that "the preaching of the cross is to them that perish foolishness; but unto us which are saved it is the power of God" (1 Cor. 1:18, KJV).

Alone and Anonymous

A few weeks ago a friend related the following incident: She was taking a course on counseling people in grief situations. One evening the instructor asked the class to break up into groups of two. Each group was to tell his or her partner the worst thing that ever happened to them. Cindy teamed up with a young woman who kept saying that something terrible had occurred in her past. She seemed overcome, but only referred to the cause of her distress in a nebulous way.

Cindy, having never lost a parent, sibling, grandparent, or anyone close to her, was at a loss to come up with an event of great sorrow in her own life. So she shared with her partner my story. Cindy told her I'd had an abortion fifteen years ago and that it had practically destroyed me, but that I had experienced forgiveness and peace through Christ.

The woman broke into tears and told Cindy, "I had an abortion too. That is the worst thing that ever happened to me! I think about it day and night. I've never told anyone and my abortion was twelve years ago."

This woman had been a Christian for several years. God's forgiveness was hers and she had never appropriated it. She was living as a pauper, denying herself all the riches of God's grace, when she was actually a child of the King.

This incident is not isolated. Whenever I tell others about my abortion, someone invariably has a tale to tell about a person who "went through hell" after an abortion. I rarely meet women who have aborted. I am sure I touch elbows with them all the time, but though I may pass within inches of them in stores, live across the street from them, or sit next to them in church, rarely do I know their identities. Over 18 million women have aborted since 1973, but for the most part we remain anonymous because abortion produces silent victims. Women who have aborted and realize their sin are often too ashamed to speak about it or are too afraid of what others will think to get the help they need.

On the other hand, some women speak of their abortions in a nonchalant way, proving they either have not considered what they really did when they aborted, or else are hiding their true emotions behind a brave display of "I don't care." One friend told me that she was at a party when the subject of abortion came up. There were ten women present and nine of them admitted having an abortion, speaking of it as something no more painful than having a wart removed. These women could speak so casually because they had not yet faced their sin. This type of emotionless response is fairly common among those who are not Christians. They do not yet realize the truth of Luke 6:25: "Woe to you who laugh now, for you shall mourn and weep."

The few women I have met who admit their abortions openly and honestly are those who have dealt with or are in the process of dealing with their abortions biblically. Even then, the tears often flow for both of us. They are tears of joy that our sin is covered by the blood of Christ and that we have found release and peace because of God's love.

Shameful Secret

Self-imposed anonymity results from one of two problems. The first is denying your feelings in order to avoid confronting them. The second is shame.

Many women are trying to deal with shame following their abortions. Sixty-five percent of those responding to my questionnaire listed shame as an emotion, often emphasizing it as one of their major hurdles in coming to terms with their abortions.

Shame occurs because of guilt, but often lingers long after the guilt has been confessed and forgiven. Romans 6:21 asks: "What benefit did you reap at that time from the things you are now ashamed of?" (NIV) There was no benefit in your abortion and your shame continues to keep you from enjoying God's forgiveness.

Shame may be what brought you to repentance. "They will loathe themselves in their own sight for the evils which they have committed" (Ezek. 6:9). Shame of your sin can have a healing effect as it steers you to repent. The Bible also tells us there is a kind of shame before God: "You will *remember your ways and be ashamed.* . . . And you shall know that I am the Lord, in order that you may *remember and be ashamed,* and never open your mouth anymore because of your humiliation, when I have *forgiven you for all that you have done*" (Ezek. 16:61-63). God spoke those words to the nation Israel, but they apply to us today. We have nothing to say in the presence of God who freely forgave that which shamed us before Him.

David pleaded to God, "Do not let me be ashamed" (Ps. 25:2, 20), but God has a new command for those who are Christians. In the New Testament Paul wrote, "Do not be ashamed of the testimony of our Lord" (2 Tim. 1:8). Dealing biblically with your past sins is a testimony to God's grace and forgiveness. People seeing you now, who have known you before, cannot fail to see that God has changed you as you yield to His teaching. Do not be ashamed of God's testimony in you.

Second Corinthians 4:1-2 says once we have renounced the hidden things of shame, we can walk before people with a clear conscience. We have hope of victory in every trial because of God's great love. "And hope maketh not ashamed; because the love of God is shed abroad in our hearts by the Holy Ghost which is given unto us" (Rom. 5:5, KJV).

Your abortion is not something to flaunt proudly as those hardened to their sin tend to do, but you must be careful you don't let shame keep you from getting the help you may need.

Facing Fear

It is interesting to note that from the survey statistics, fear is one of only two negative emotions that *decreased* following abortion. The primary reason for this, I believe, is that the reason for your fear—your untimely pregnancy—was gone. Gone were your fears of having to bear an illegitimate child, gone the fear of having to drop out of school or change your career, gone the fear of having to admit you had committed adultery, gone was the unknown child whose presence you feared enough to kill him.

However, since over half (54 percent) of the women responding to my questionnaire listed fear as a problem, we know that though the original fears lessened, new fears emerged. What is it you now fear? Do you fear pregnancy and so avoid a proper relationship with your husband? Do you fear hospitals or doctors because of your abortion experience? Do you fear having to face abortion and its relation to you personally? Do you fear rejection if someone were to discover your secret?

Fear takes two distinct forms. Fear of God, or reverential fear, is healthy and necessary if we are to live as God desires. "The fear of the Lord is the beginning of knowledge; fools despise wisdom and instruction" (Prov. 1:7; 9:10; Ps. 111:10). Reverential fear of God does not mean you should view God as some giant standing over you with a whip. Our God is loving and our fear of Him should be an awe at the wonder of His greatness and love for each of us in spite of our sins against Him. Proper fear of the Lord will keep you from evil (Prov. 16:6). When we permit sin to exist in our lives, we know our fear of God is diminished, because proper fear inhibits sins (Ps. 25:12).

Unless you fear God in a respectful, reverential way, you will not have success in overcoming the second type of fear, which manifests itself in anticipation of what someone or something can do to you. "The fear of man bringeth a snare, but whoso putteth his trust in the Lord shall be safe" (Prov. 29:25, KJV). Your fears can be overcome by placing your confidence in God.

Again, God leaves the choice of whom we will fear up to us. If we choose to fear God, He requires that we please Him. "Seek first His kingdom and His righteousness; and all these things shall be added unto you" (Matt. 6:33). No matter how great our fear, God says to please Him we must obey His Word. He gives us the reason in Colossians 1:10: "So that you may walk in a manner worthy of the Lord, to please Him in all respects, bearing fruit in every good work and increasing in the knowledge of God."

Realize too that not all fear of man is sinful. God has given us a healthy sense of fear to know what to stay away from. This healthy fear would more appropriately be termed *caution*. However, the majority of our fears result from sinful responses to trying situations.

Getting Rid of Fear
Have your fears so encompassed you that you are willing to do *anything* to rid yourself of them? Such an attitude only encourages your fear. Rather, you need to take the attitude, I will be willing to do anything *God* wants me to do to rid myself of this fear.[1] Remember, you must seek God *first* (Matt. 6:33). If you put

ridding your fear first, you will surely fail, for that is not God's way. But beware of turning to Him merely to rid yourself of your fear. God knows your motives and your heart. You can overcome your fear only when you keep your eyes on Christ.

Matthew 14:25-31 records the incident of Peter walking on the water. As he began to walk, he took his eyes off Christ and, looking toward the stormy sky, became afraid. He began to sink, and cried out, "Lord, save me!" Jesus reached out His hand and saved Peter, admonishing him, "O you of little faith, why did you doubt?"

Do you doubt God can overcome your fear? Don't. He is the God of the impossible. "For *nothing* will be impossible with God" (Luke 1:37).

The first step in resolving your fear is to make a list of what you fear most. What have you neglected doing because of your fear? For example, do you need to correct a sexual relation with your husband regardless of your fear? That was one of my primary problems. I feared pregnancy to such an extent that our sexual relations were few and far between. My fear was causing me to defraud my husband of a rightful relationship. It was hard to set my mind on pleasing God by risking pregnancy. I was so afraid. What is it you need to do to please God?

I can almost hear you saying, "But I'm too afraid to try it!" Consider Daniel for a moment (Dan. 6). Here is a person who had every reason to fear. He continued to pray to God three times each day in direct contradiction to the king's edict which forbade worship to anyone but himself. The penalty was death. But Daniel revered God more than he feared the king. Don't you think Daniel might have been just a little fearful of being thrown to the lions, which was the penalty for disobeying the king? Daniel did what God wanted—and took the consequences of disobeying the law. Daniel trusted God to protect him in that pit filled with starving lions. He came through that trial alive and well.

Likewise, God goes before you into any situation in which *He* asks you to become involved. He may ask you to go where you are most afraid because He wants to show you that He alone can see you through your fears. When you obey the Lord, He will honor your obedience.

Our God is a God of love and assures us that "perfect love casts out fear" (1 John 4:18). Love is stronger than fear and is the force that overpowers fear. "For God has not given us the spirit of fear,

but of power, and of love and of a sound mind" (2 Tim. 1:7, KJV).
We have God's power, Christ's love, and the Holy Spirit's guidance telling us to do what is right. Love focuses on others as it
looks for ways to give, to meet another's needs.

In contrast, fear focuses on me. How can *I* keep from being
involved? How will it affect *me*? *I'm* so afraid to try! You are
responsible for your response to fear, just as you are responsible
for all your thoughts and actions (Ezek. 18:20).

To overcome your fear, you must focus on the loving thing that
God requires of you, whatever it may be. Dwell on the benefit
you can bring to someone else. Do not dwell on your fear. Realize
you might have your fears actualized as you obey God. Commit
yourself to God and claim 1 Corinthians 10:13. Your fear will
diminish in direct proportion to your obedience to God's commands regarding that which you fear. Then, one day you will find
yourself gladly doing the thing which you once feared. God is
asking you to trust Him.

> When you lie down, you will not be afraid; when you lie
> down, your sleep will be sweet. Do not be afraid of
> sudden fear, nor of the onslaught of the wicked when it
> comes; for the Lord will be your confidence, and will
> keep your foot from being caught (Prov. 3:24-26).

Why Worry?
Do you worry about someone finding out about your abortion?
Do you worry about whether you can have another baby? What
do you worry about? Like fear, women expressed more problems
with the emotion of anxiety or worry before their abortions. The
reason for this is probably that following the abortion, most of us
felt a false sense of relief over a situation we thought to be settled
once and for all. Now new worries have crept in.

Worry is concern over the future, over something which you
can do nothing about. Worry comes from a Greek word, *merim-
nao*,[2] that means "to tear apart." And that is just what worry does
to a person. It tears them apart inside, for worry is an internal
emotion. You control worry, but worry can often get the better
of you and manifest itself in physical ailments such as ulcers.
Worry also affects your looks. "Anxiety in the heart of a man
weighs it down" (Prov. 12:25). Matthew 6:34 commands us, "Do
not be anxious for tomorrow; for tomorrow will care for itself.

Each day has enough trouble of its own." Worry is sin because by worrying, you display a lack of trust in God.

It is important to understand that worrying is different from planning. James 4:13-15 speaks of planning for the future with the understanding that all plans are subject to God's sovereign will. We can plan without worrying. "The mind of a man plans his way, but the Lord directs his steps" (Prov. 16:9). "Commit your works to the Lord, and your plans will be established" (Prov. 16:3). Planning ahead can eliminate worry in many cases.

God will never leave us nor forsake us (Heb. 13:5). Worry denies this truth as it looks inwardly to what will happen *to* me rather than upwardly to what wonderful things God has planned *for* me. Keep in mind Romans 8:28: "All things work together for good" (KJV). Worry denies this also, for it assumes some things in our lives will not work for good. Worry says, "I believe God, but what if. . . ?"

Have you ever heard the story of Mary and Martha? Jesus had come to visit these two sisters. Martha was busy preparing dinner while Mary sat at Jesus' feet. Martha said, "Lord, do You not care that my sister has left me to do all the serving alone? Then tell her to help me."

But the Lord answered her, "Martha, Martha, you are *worried* and bothered about so many things; but only a few things are necessary, really only one, for Mary has chosen the good part, which shall not be taken away from her" (Luke 10:40-42).

You see, Mary had chosen to obey the Lord and to seek Him. Martha was so worried about everything else that she missed the blessing God had for her. She could have prepared a simple meal and had time to sit at Jesus' feet also, but her eyes were on what others would think of her. She spent her time preparing an elaborate meal, all the while worrying about "so many things."

The cure for worry is found in Philippians 4. "Be anxious for nothing, but in everything by prayer and supplication with thanksgiving let your requests be made known to God" (Phil. 4:6). God commands us not to worry, but instead, to bring everything to Him in prayer, thanking Him for working in our lives. If you follow the instructions in verse 6, God will give you peace (v. 7).

"Finally, brethren, whatever is true, whatever is honorable, whatever is right, whatever is pure, whatever is lovely, whatever is of good repute, if there is any excellence and if anything worthy of praise, let your mind dwell on these things" (v. 8). If we set our minds to think as God instructs us to, and then if we do what He tells us to, worry won't stand a chance!

We can learn to be content with our circumstances, whatever they are (v. 11). Then we can claim Philippians 4:13 as our own promise from God: "I can do all things through Him who strengthens me." This verse will not only help you conquer worry, but it will help you in resolving all your problems regarding your abortion, as well as anything else that you will encounter in life.

Philippians 4:19 says, "And my God shall supply all your needs according to His riches in glory in Christ Jesus." If God wants you to have another baby, you will. If God's best interests will be served by others knowing about your abortion, He will meet your emotional needs at that time. Why worry now? We don't know what God has planned for us and worrying only robs us of the joy we should have in living for God today.

Claim these promises as your own as you live one day at a time: "Casting all your anxiety upon Him, because He cares for you" (1 Peter 5:7). "Cast your burden upon the Lord and He will sustain you; He will never allow the righteous to be shaken" (Ps. 55:22).

God does care about you and wants to take care of you and your every need. He will sustain you through each day. Trust God and—don't worry!

Would Someone Please Listen?

Women who have aborted are caught between a burning desire to vocalize their feelings and a fearful reluctance to confide in anyone. Seventy-eight percent of those surveyed said they felt a *need* to talk with someone. However, when we do decide we *must* talk, finding someone to talk to is not always easy.

Women who have aborted in secret are not about to shout it from the rooftops or even to whisper it behind closed doors. We want to forget about it. But pushing the fact you have aborted into the deep recesses of your mind and refusing to think about it only compounds your problems. As we have seen, your emotions must be dealt with in order for you to be free. You can't deal with your abortion if you refuse to think and talk about it.

Husbands and friends can play a valuable role by being available to listen. Even though they cannot fully comprehend what you have been through, a sensitive listening ear can help you to verbally sort out your feelings so you can begin to deal with them in a way pleasing to God.

But what I longed for was someone with whom I could talk about my abortion without having to go into the grisly details and yet who would know exactly what I was talking about. The only person to fit that requirement was another woman who had experienced abortion. Only someone who had walked in my shoes could truly understand. I waited twelve years to find such a friend. Just knowing there really was someone else who had aborted and had survived made a lot of difference in realizing I was not alone in my feelings.

As I began research for this book, I discovered that organizations exist nationwide for the purpose of helping women deal with abortion's aftermath (see Appendix A). Women who are or were hurting have let themselves be known in an unselfish effort to aid others, who like themselves, have had abortions. They get together and discuss problems they now face and ways of dealing with them.

When talking with other women who have aborted, you must take care not to let your emotions cause you to sin. You can express your distress over having aborted without blameshifting or bitterness. Likewise, you must not permit the venom of others to contaminate you. Women who do not know Christ as their personal Saviour, or who have not had any experience using the Scriptures to solve their emotional conflicts, may view talking as an avenue of release for pent-up anger or guilt. You can help these women by quietly telling them that you are resolving your abortion aftermath biblically. God may present an opportunity for you to tell someone about Christ and gently lead them to the only cure for their sins. What a privilege that would be!

Perhaps you do not know anyone in whom you can confide. You may be single, far from family and friends, or totally alone with the knowledge that you aborted. Remember that God Himself is always waiting to hear from you and will listen to *every* word. He wants to see you healed more than any person on this earth. God will take your tears and turn them into joy (Ps. 30:5). He will take your fear and show you how to have peace; your bitterness He will change into love (Col. 3:12-16).

However, if you believe you need professional help in dealing with your abortion, you need to carefully select a counselor. Biblical counseling centers are available. However, if anyone at any time tells you to correct your problems by a means contrary to what God says in the Bible, do not take their advice. The Bible is the only place where you can find permanent and complete answers to your problems. Anything else will further frustrate you.

Regardless of whether you seek counsel, do not neglect to talk with the Great Counselor. He'll always listen!

A Lingering Fear

Perhaps you are afraid to talk about your abortion. Is it because you have been present when abortion was being discussed, and have heard people referring to women who abort as "cruel, heartless, baby killers"? Do you die a little inside when you hear such statements? Do you wonder what people would say if they knew you were one of those "monsters"?

Most people, when speaking of women who have aborted as a general group, tend to refer to them in accusatory tones. However, from personal experience, I have found that these same people, when made aware that I had experienced an abortion, usually look upon me with compassion for what I have undergone. There is a big difference in people's minds between "women who have aborted" and knowing a particular woman who has aborted. Knowing the person makes all the difference in feelings toward them. It shouldn't be true, but it is.

Yet some people whom you know will treat you with contempt once they know about your abortion. Expect it. Accept it. It is even possible your pastor may attempt to put you on a further guilt trip if you seek his counseling. If he does, find another counselor!

Abortion is *not* the unpardonable sin. And you must accept the unforgiving people as they are, regardless of their treatment or feelings toward you. You can best help such a person by showing them in word and in deed that you are not the same woman you were when you aborted. Your life has changed for the better because of the struggles you have had in resolving your guilt. As hard as it will be, God tells us to love others who may have unloving attitudes toward us (Rom. 12:17-21).

And remember—the other person may have a skeleton in his closet that is worse than yours!

ELEVEN

Aching Associates

During an untimely pregnancy, the woman and those who know about her situation suffer as she deliberates her course of action. It would seem the loving thing to do would be to remedy the immediate problem—the pregnancy. When I was considering abortion, people close to me saw how I was suffering over what to do—I was single, in college, financially dependent upon my parents, and emotionally upset. I know some of these people truly suffered out of compassion for me. Out of love they sought to resolve my dilemma by encouraging me to abort. So many times people see abortion as the loving solution to a woman's sincere distress over an untimely pregnancy. The woman may be poor, single, physically ill, or emotionally upset. People reach out in "love" to assist her to rid herself of her problem. They do this either by remaining silent so as not to force their personal beliefs on the woman, or else by encouraging her she is doing the "right" thing by aborting.

That isn't God's love as revealed in the Bible. God's love says that we are to help the person become all that God desires them to be, and that this is accomplished by working with the person *through* the problem, not by rushing them off to remove their problem. God's love says that suffering mustn't always be eliminated. Love is keeping the hurt you feel to yourself as you reach out to do what is best for another person.

Family Responses
I have never discussed my abortion with my brothers and sister. However, I did write to them to find out how they felt at that time

and now. Looking back, they feel that abortion was the best for me because of my situation. They see that it allowed me to continue my life unhindered by a child out of wedlock. Yet their letters state that while they do not think about the nephew they never knew, they are searching personally for answers to the problem of abortion.

As I was preparing this manuscript, I heard from a woman whose sister had an abortion. This woman is a Christian and aches for the nephew or niece she will never know. She admits that she had mixed feelings at the time of the abortion, but she didn't try to stop it. She considered the situation her sister was in and kept silent. Today this woman regrets her silence and remains bitter toward physicians and counselors who encourage abortions.

This brings us to the fact that a woman does not accomplish abortion on her own. She must have assistance, if not in the realm of counseling, then ultimately in the physical removal of her baby from her body. If no person could be found to perform the abortion, we would bear our babies, or learn to refrain from activities which cause untimely pregnancies. We were not alone when we aborted, but still we should not harbor grudges against those who willingly complied with our request. We are victims of our own choosing, of our own selfishness. Other people hurt because we have committed the sin of abortion.

In discussing aching associates, there are many possibilities. Perhaps one of your parents knows and the other doesn't. Maybe neither knows; maybe both know and you think they don't. Maybe they both know because you told them prior to or after the fact. Possibly your husband or boyfriend doesn't know. Maybe no one knows; or maybe everybody knows.

In the case of parents or others close to you not knowing, the problem arises that you are faced with keeping your abortion a secret. This poses difficulties when the topic of abortion arises in general conversation. As we've discussed, it's hard to listen to talk of abortion as you silently suffer. On the other hand, it's uncomfortable to remain silent when you want to express honest feelings now that you are coming to terms with your abortion. If people *do* know about you, you have the worry of someone letting your secret slip. Secrets of this type may eventually become more of a problem than telling the truth openly, and if others are involved in your secret, you impose on them an awesome responsibility, especially if they are having trouble dealing with your abortion also.

My parents knew about my abortion. Because of that they have suffered fifteen years over their decision to let me have my own way. They too lovingly wrote to me at my request to share their thoughts about my abortion. I have never discussed my abortion in-depth with them because I believed they were still hurting and that discussing it would hurt them more. I merely told them I knew I had sinned and asked their forgiveness.

However, when presented with my questions, Mom and Dad talked for hours with each other about my abortion and its effect on them. Apparently, they had never really talked it out before between themselves. They wrote:

> In the beginning we did talk about the abortion, but gradually we kept our thoughts to ourselves . . . [Pam] has found more peace since starting her book and we in turn have opened up to each other and the other children to discuss this and it has also brought us peace. We know God has forgiven us too as we were not strong enough to change her mind.

Then they add the part that haunts so many people who have participated in an abortion: "We cannot forgive ourselves."

How thankful I am that my letter opened the door for my parents to begin to resolve their emotional conflicts. That they have forgiven me is a fact I cannot fathom, just as I cannot understand how God could forgive so great a sin.

As I have done, so too my parents must come to terms with the abortion before God. All the solutions to my emotional conflicts will work for them also. Perhaps as time goes on, I will have opportunities to show them what God says regarding guilt and remorse. The first move must be mine, for the cause of their pain is my responsibility. I aborted their grandchild.

On the other hand, sometimes parents do not know about an abortion beforehand. They may never know about it. Other parents may have known about the abortion and condoned it at the time. They may now regret their decision and their encouragement or their part in arranging for an "easy" solution to an untimely pregnancy. Sometimes parents become estranged from their daughters because of abortion. Parents have feelings too.

They may be bitter against you, or they may harbor no ill feelings. You may inadvertently have placed a wall between yourself and your parents because of your own guilt.

Men's Reactions

Because of our laws, fathers of unborn children do not have a say in whether the baby is aborted (*Planned Parenthood vs. Danforth*, 1976). When we speak of personal rights, we have sadly neglected the father in the instance of an untimely pregnancy. True, in many cases the father does not want the child, does not intend to support it nor to marry its mother. Our laws act to the benefit of men who have this mindset. Though they are also responsible for the pregnancy, men are free to walk away from the situation. Kennedy speaks well to this when he says that leaving the decision to the woman and her doctor

> leaves the husband and prospective father out of the problem altogether, freeing him from something for which he has just as much responsibility as the woman, even if we restrict our understanding of it to the basic biological facts. But this question entails a great deal more than just biology; it includes some of the most solemn issues involved in being a person. Among these are the nature and demands of mature relationships between men and women, the shape and future of marriage and the family, the nature of love, and the power of certain professional people in the most intimate areas of our lives. To place all the burden for a decision about abortion on the woman is to separate her from her relationship to man.[1]

Kennedy goes on to explain that negating the man's wishes in the abortion issue gives the man an undeserved sense of freedom. It also distorts the basic relation of husband and wife which involves consequences for our joint actions. The man walks away and the woman finds herself alone.

Conversely, sometimes a man *does* want his unborn child, while the woman wants to abort it. The law works to the detriment of the father in these instances. How ridiculous is a law that protects the irresponsible and ties the hands of those men who desire to assume the responsibility that is rightfully theirs. Thus, men find themselves in a position of watching at the sidelines as the woman destroys a part of them. After all, a child is formed from the union of an egg from the female and a sperm from the male. The unborn child is just as much the man's as it is the woman's.

I have spoken to and have received letters from men who wanted the babies they sired. Regardless of their wishes, the woman aborted the baby. These men are now left with an emptiness that the woman herself may not yet feel. One man states:

> Of course, being male, I don't know what right I have to impose my views on a subject whose full scope I could never grasp. [I felt] absolutely helpless—it was out of my hands.

Some men whose girlfriends aborted later married that same woman. Together some of these couples have "gone through hell," as one man wrote, trying to reconcile their joint decision. Though the woman had the abortion, the baby was lost to both of them. Sometimes the bond between such a couple grows stronger as they resolve their emotional conflicts together, as Christians, drawing upon Christ's healing love. Other marriages have ended in divorce because the act of abortion has separated the partners as each recoiled into himself or herself in an unsuccessful attempt to forget.

For many of us, the man to whom we are presently married was not the father of our aborted baby. He may know about us, or he may not know, depending upon our willingness to open ourselves to our spouse. My husband knows about me, indeed, knew about me prior to our marriage. I asked his thoughts and this is what he wrote:

> Abortion only affected me indirectly. Since it was not my child and I was only related to the situation after the fact, the only effect was concerning my wife's reaction to [the abortion]. However, at the time I was still somewhat indifferent towards the idea of abortion. It affected our relationship when she was unable to come to grips with the guilt and ill feelings that began to come. . . . Concerning sex, there was always the fear of pregnancy because further children were not wanted—

I don't know if I really knew what the reason for this was. However, many different methods of birth control were used, with great fear of their failure, and thus sex was difficult and strained.

Though Leigh never participated in my abortion in any way, he too bore the pain as he watched me go through its aftermath. My abortion affected him more deeply than I will ever know, as he struggled to help me pull myself together. He lived my nightmares as though they were his own, being there to hold and to comfort me in my anguish. For us, the years of abortion aftermath brought us closer together.

Siblings

One last group of people remains to be considered in the abortion aftermath. As I write this chapter, my thoughts go to my own three living children. What will they think when they one day discover that Mom killed their half-brother? Will they wonder why he died when they were permitted to live? Will they love me less? How will my abortion affect them?

I hope and pray they will see it was a sin which I have confessed and been forgiven of before God. I hope they will learn from my mistake that all life is sacred and that the time of death is rightly God's choice. I trust my children will learn that women are to be respected and that sex is for marriage because of the sacredness of the union and because children may be produced by the act of intercourse. I pray my children will not be deeply hurt by my selfish actions. Because they are young and my abortion was so long ago, they may be spared the trauma of abortion affecting them personally.

However, what about the children who were living at the time their mother aborted? Perhaps the woman aborted in order to maintain the family's standard of living. What will those children think when they realize they were spared, perhaps simply because they were conceived at the "right" time while their sibling's life was terminated because of the inopportune time of his conception? Those children who were permitted to live must come to realize sooner or later that they live because they were wanted. Wantedness once again assumes an important role in life as these children struggle to determine what makes one wanted. They may live only because they were the right sex—Mommy wanted a boy and the tests determined they were male. Or they may wonder if they were spared because at the time of their conception abortion was illegal. Had it been legal, would their mothers have aborted them also? These are questions that may plague the minds of children, even very young children, as they realize their moms limited the family size by resorting to murder.

Dr. Phillip Ney, head of the Department of Psychological Medicine at Christchurch Clinical School, New Zealand, considers newborns as abortion survivors. He states:

> When up to 50 percent of North American pregnancies end by induced abortion, it is reasonable to consider a live newborn as a survivor. In any situation where a mother, spouse, grandparents, or physician has seriously deliberated abortion, the live child has survived a carefully considered option to destroy him.[2]

How will these children cope with abortion in their lives?

Where Will It End?

Abortion is not an isolated act. By its very nature it involves numerous people, many of whom we may not know personally. When we aborted, the act itself rippled out in ever widening waves, encompassing innocent people in its wake. Even if you have managed to keep your abortion a secret, even if your parents, husband, and close friends do not know, the aftermath continues to grow. Somewhere along the line someone has been forever changed by your act. It may be a nurse who treated you. It may be a friend who aborted because you did and seemed to come through it "OK." It may be your boyfriend who unknowingly was a father for a few short weeks. It may be a parent who never knew the joy of a grandchild. These people were shortchanged.

You and I have changed the course of history as we destroyed children that may have gone on to become leaders or laborers, and the parents of future generations of children. Only God knows what the future may have been had over 18 million children been permitted to live over the last thirteen years.

Others are aching, and we must go to those whom we can and in love help them to reconcile their emotional turmoil over our abortions. We who have aborted must now be the ones to reach

out in compassion and understanding. Only when all is recon-
ciled as far as we are able, may we then live in peace.

T W E L V E

Achieving Abundant Living

This book was written to focus your attention on your personal guilt in aborting and then to assist you to begin to deal with the resultant aftermath. There are no easy answers when you have had an abortion. Your life has been irrevocably changed. Abortion, unlike other sins, has no means of recompense. That is part of the problem with abortion. The act is final.

Think about a thief. When someone steals, he or she may be caught and may have to pay the price of their crime by serving time in prison. When the person is released, they are free to carry on with their life. They may even be able to make restitution by repaying some or all of that which they stole. Then they can get on with their lives, truly leaving their sin in their past.

For us who have aborted, though we never serve time in jail, the self-imposed sentence we serve amounts to life imprisonment within our tortured minds. Unlike the thief, we cannot repay in any way that which we took. Life can never be given back once taken. And ultimately, though we may become Christians and reconcile ourselves before God and people, we live daily with a sin which is ever present before our eyes.

The simple fact is that you never "get over" an abortion. Though it is the most common elective surgical procedure in America today, abortion leaves a woman infected with an oozing abscess of emotional turmoil that refuses to go away. As you have seen, Christ is the only answer to your pain. Applying biblical principles to your life in order to resolve your emotional conflicts is the only process whereby you may be healed from that pain.

But though the wound can heal, the scars will be with you throughout your life. One woman writes, "Abortion is not something you do and then just forget about it. I tried blocking it from my mind but it is something I will always remember. God has forgiven me but it is a part of my life."[1] God graciously forgives, but allows our memories to remain, perhaps as a reminder of His great love to us.

You may not believe it now, but as time goes on and as you deal with your emotions according to God's methods, your memories of your abortion will grow dimmer. But be advised, there is only one way to deal with the guilt, anger, bitterness, frustration, and all the other emotions churning within you. To permanently resolve your conflicts, you must study what God has to say and then apply His Word to your life.

There is a portion of Scripture which reads:

> Not that I have already obtained it, or have already become perfect, but I press on in order that I may lay hold of that for which also I was laid hold of by Christ Jesus. Brethren, I do not regard myself as having laid hold of it yet; but one thing I do: forgetting what lies behind and reaching forward to what lies ahead, I press on toward the goal for the prize of the upward call of God in Christ Jesus (Phil. 3:12-14).

Those words were written by Paul, a man who, prior to his conversion, persecuted Christians mercilessly (Gal. 1:13). He stood over the body of Stephen, as that first Christian martyr was stoned to death (Acts 7:58; 8:1—Saul was Paul's name before his conversion). Paul entered the homes of Christians and dragged them off to prison for their faith (Acts 8:3). Indeed, he was on his way to Damascus to capture more Christians when he was confronted by Christ and converted (Acts 9:1-19). Yet Paul, responsible for the deaths of innocent people, embraced a new goal which was "the prize of the upward call of God in Christ Jesus." That must be our goal if we are to forget the past.

Paul did not say that he literally forgot his past sins. Actually, he recalled them in Galatians, for instance, showing he still remembered that which he had done to offend God. But in this passage from Philippians Paul is saying that we should not dwell on our sins, but realize they are in the past. Then we can move forward to those things which God has for us to accomplish for Him today.

Practically speaking, you may be asking, "But what about the pictures and words that confront me daily? How can I forget?"

After my abortion, I found it virtually impossible *not* to look at the pictures which so vividly show a fetus looking like the person he is. Yet for a long time, I would cry whenever I saw one of these pictures. Finally, I determined to pray each time I came across one of these reminders of my sin. Now, as I look on an innocent life taken in misconception, I pray to God and thank Him for the fact that Christ paid the price for my sin and that I am no longer guilty of that sin. I ask God to remove the pain of my abortion and to permit me to read and see and discuss the topic to His glory without emotional trauma to me.

I pray that the thousands of women who will consider abortion these next few months may decide to keep their babies. I pray that the immorality that leads to the vast majority of unwanted pregnancies will cease. And I pray that God will heal the millions of women who have aborted and have yet to find the answer to their pain.

I've determined to meet the problem of abortion in my life and in the lives of others in God's way—without shame, or bitterness, or anger. That is how I deal with seeing constant reminders of my abortion. I give all my pain to Christ, who intercedes on my behalf before the Father in heaven (Heb. 7:25).

Tom Constable wrote the following words in his article, "Is Prayer Optional?"

> We desperately need God's help. His Word says so, our experience says so, and the challenges we face say so. May God impress each of us with how desperately we need Him so that we feel driven to pray.[2]

The saying, "God helps those who help themselves" sounds good, but it isn't biblical and it won't work. The truth is that God helps those who admit they can't help themselves and lean totally on His power as they work through their problems.

> Come to Me, all who are weary and heavy-laden, and I will give you rest. Take My yoke upon you, and learn from Me, for I am gentle and humble in heart; and you

shall find rest for your souls. For My yoke is easy, and
My load is light (Matt. 11:28-30).

When you have had an abortion and realize the enormity of
your sin you become heavy-laden with guilt and remorse. Christ
tells you to cast *all* your burdens upon Him. Let Him bear the
weight of your abortion. Once you are a Christian, the weight of
your sin is no longer yours to bear. That burden now belongs to
Christ.

It would be a lie for me to tell you that I never hurt when I
think of my abortion. I do. And sometimes I cry when I discuss
the topic. That's OK. It shows others that I do have feelings, that I
care very much about abortion and its effects on women. In the
beginning, when I first began to deal with my emotions, I found
myself topsy-turvy—one day "up" and the next day "down."
Healing takes time, and the length of time depends a great deal on
your willingness to live according to God's commands.

When you find yourself in a situation where the topic of abortion comes up, you may be tempted to speak flippantly of your
abortion as other women do. Never let it appear you take your
abortion lightly. It was a grave sin and God receives the glory
only when you speak of your abortion in truth and in love. As
opportunities present themselves, let people see that abortion
has affected you, that you are not the same woman because of it.
Keeping secret the fact that abortion produces second victims
only helps perpetuate the lie that abortion is an "easy out."

Obviously, to avoid abortion the problem must be dealt with at
its root, which is the sin of illicit sex producing unwanted conception. We women must learn to revere our bodies as God does.
We must refrain from the pleasure of sin. Just as immorality is the
root of the problem, the heart of the matter is that people no
longer regard children as gifts from the Lord.

In 1971 when I aborted, I was so *grateful* I was living in New
York State where abortion was available at the woman's whim.
Little did I realize that my gratitude was to be short-lived as I
began to grapple with the truth regarding my act. Today it hardly
seems possible that I should have been so deceived, by others as
well as in my own mind, that I would have murdered my first
child. While I am not proud of my sin, I do thank God for my past.
However, I rejoice that it *is* past.

Luke 7:37-50 relates the story of a woman who is described

simply as "a sinner." When she heard Jesus was in the city, she brought costly perfume which she mingled with her tears as she anointed His feet. This act of love cost the woman time, money, and most importantly, her self-respect as the onlookers insulted and rebuked her. But this woman loved Christ more than words can tell because she knew the freedom of sins forgiven. Verse 47 reads:

> For this reason I [Jesus] say to you, her sins, which are many, have been forgiven, for she loved much.

That's me too—forgiven, cleansed, and serving God. And God can and will use *you.* You are a cleansed vessel, now fit for the Master's use. Permit God to use you through your suffering to tell others of His truth and love. Tell others they can also be forgiven, that they don't have to live in their past, but can face a bright future.

Sometimes things do get worse before they get better. "Weeping may endure for a night, but joy cometh in the morning" (Ps. 30:5, KJV). Others have traveled the long, dark tunnel of suffering following abortion, but have emerged into the light of day to live once again in the sunshine. Experience 1 Corinthians 10:13 for yourself. Now let others see the Son shine in you!

John Peterson has written a song that thrills my soul when I sing it and realize the heart-healing truth of the words. It is my prayer that one day soon you can sing it from *your* heart:

> Gone is the guilt of my sin,
> Peace is now reigning within;
> Since I believed—pardon received
> Happy, so happy I've been.
> New life in Christ, abundant and free!
> What glories shine, what joys are mine,
> What wondrous blessings I see!
> My past with its sin, the searching and strife,
> Forever gone—there's a bright new dawn!
> For in Christ I have found new life![3]

Appendix A

Help Groups for Aborted Women

OPEN ARMs (Abortion-Related Ministries)
National Headquarters
P.O. Box 7188
Federal Way, Washington 98003
(206) 352-7228

PACE INC. (Post Abortion Counseling and
Education)
P.O. Box 35032
Tucson, Arizona 85740
(602) 742-5835

WEBA (Women Exploited by Abortion)
National Headquarters
P.O. Box 267
Schoolcraft, Michigan 49087
(616) 679-4069

Helpful Reading on Healing
Damaged Emotions

Christ and Your Problems, Jay E. Adams,
1971
Presbyterian & Reformed Publishing Co.
P.O. Box 817, Phillipsburg, NJ 08865

Godliness through Discipline, Jay E. Adams,
1972
Presbyterian & Reformed Publishing Co.
P.O. Box 817, Phillipsburg, NJ 08865

Healing for Damaged Emotions, David
Seamands, 1981
Victor Books
P.O. Box 1825, Wheaton, IL 60189

The Healing of the Mind
Faith and Life Publications
632 N. Prosperity Lane, Andover, KS 67002

For Further Reading on Life Before Birth

Who Broke the Baby? Jean Stalker Garton, 1979
Minneapolis: Bethany Fellowship Inc.

The Right to Live, The Right to Die, C. Everett Koop, 1982
Wheaton, Ill.: Tyndale House Publishers, Inc.

Abortion and the Conscience of the Nation, Ronald Reagan, 1984
New York: Thomas Nelson Publishers

Rites of Life, Landrum Shettles and David Rorvik, 1983
Grand Rapids: Zondervan

Handbook on Abortion, John Willke, 1979
Cincinnati, Ohio: Hayes Publishing Company

Appendix B

I am preparing a book designed to help women who have had an abortion to deal with the emotional aftermath they face. If you have had an abortion (or know someone who has), the answers to the following questions would be of assistance to me in this work. Answering the questions may cause painful memories, but if you are able to put your thoughts to paper, it will be greatly appreciated. Please omit your name and address. Please feel free to use additional paper for your responses if necessary.

1. How old were you when you had your abortion? How old are you now?
2. How many abortions have you had?
3. Were you married at the time?
4. Are you married now?
5. Do you have other children?
6. Were they born prior to or following the abortion?
7. What is your religious background?
8. Was your abortion legal? If so, would you have consented to an illegal abortion?
9. How many weeks pregnant were you at the time of your abortion?
10. What method of abortion was used?
11. What was your emotional reaction immediately after the abortion?
12. Do your spouse/family/parents know about the abortion?
13. What is the specific reason you chose to have an abortion?
14. Did anyone help you in your decision? Who? (E.g., parents, spouse, pastor, doctor, etc.)
15. Would you consent to another abortion? For what reasons?
16. Do you believe what you did was wrong?
17. Did you ever have trouble "coming to grips" with what you had done?
18. Is the topic of abortion painful for you to discuss or read about?
19. What feelings do you have when you read an article or see pictures dealing with abortion?

20. Do you ever feel the need to talk to someone about the abortion?
21. Did you seek counsel following your abortion?
22. Circle the emotions you had PRIOR to your abortion:
    anger, anxiety, bitterness, blame-shifting, depression, doubt, fear, frustration, guilt, hope, indignation, peace, remorse, resentfulness, righteousness, self-pity, shame, other _____
23. Circle the emotions you have had SINCE your abortion:
    anger, anxiety, bitterness, blame-shifting, depression, doubt, fear, freedom, frustration, grief, guilt, hope, indignation, peace, remorse, repentance, resentfulness, righteousness, self-pity, shame, other _____
24. What are your feelings RIGHT NOW, after having filled out this questionnaire?
25. Are there any additional thoughts you wish to share?

Thank you for your willingness to share your thoughts with me.

Notes

Chapter 4—Abortion American Style

[1]*Statistical Abstract of the U.S. 1985,* 105th ed. (Washington, D.C.: U.S. Bureau of the Census, 1983), p. 67.

[2]Dr. and Mrs. J.C. Willke, *Handbook on Abortion* (Cincinnati: Hiltz Publishing Co., 1972), p. 45.

[3]C. Everett Koop, *The Right to Live, The Right to Die* (Wheaton, IL: Tyndale House, 1982), p. 61.

[4]Landrum Shettles and David Rorvik, *Rites of Life* (Grand Rapids: Zondervan, 1983), p. 118.

[5]Koop, *op. cit,* p. 60.

[6]Betty Benjamin, "The Case for Pro-Choice," *Should Abortions Be Permitted?* ed. David L. Bender (St. Paul, MN: Greenhaven Press, n.d.), p. 94.

[7]Patti McKinney in "WEBA: Voice of Experience Relates Horror of Abortion," by Deborah W. Huff.

[8]*Webster's New World Dictionary,* college ed. (New York: World Publishing Co., 1966), p. 257. All future dictionary references are from this source unless otherwise noted.

[9]Quoted by Helen Epstein, "Abortion: An Issue That Won't Go Away," *New York Times Magazine* (March 30, 1980). Note: In the early 1960s, Planned Parenthood stated that abortion "kills the life of the baby" in their literature. They now operate abortion clinics throughout the U.S.

[10]Susan Deller Ross and Ann Barcher, *The Rights of Women* (Toronto: Bantam Books, 1973), p. 179.

[11]Jill Lessard in Huff, *op. cit.*

[12]Jean Stalker Garton, *Who Broke the Baby?* (Minneapolis: Bethany Fellowship, 1979), p. 45.

[13]Elisabeth Elliot, "When I Was Being Made in Secret" (Westchester, IL: Good News Publishers, n.d.).

[14]Bernard Nathanson with Richard Ostling, *Aborting America* (New York: Pinnacle Books, 1979), p. 197.

[15]*Centers for Disease Control Abortion Surveillance,* U.S. Department of Health and Human Services: Atlanta, May 1983, p. 58.

[16]David Granfield, *The Abortion Decision* (Garden City, NY: Doubleday & Co., 1969), p. 84.

[17]Susan Deller Ross and Ann Barcher, *The Rights of Women* (Toronto: Bantam Books, 1973), p. 183.

[18]See "What We Didn't Understand" for details.

[19]"Pro Life Medical Survey," editorial, *About Issues* (November 1982), p. 42.

[20]Lippis, *op. cit,* p. 17.

[21]John M. Frame, "Abortion from a Biblical Perspective," *Thou Shalt Not Kill,* ed. Richard L. Ganz (New Rochelle, NY: Arlington House, 1978), p. 74.

[22]Claire Chambers, *The Siecus Circle: A Humanist Revolution* (Belmont, MA: Western Islands, 1977), p. 321.

[23]*Ibid.*

[24]David LaFontaine, "The Case for Pro Life," *Should Abortions Be Permitted?* ed. David L. Bender (St. Paul, MN: Greenhaven Press, n.d.), p. 94.

[25]Dr. and Mrs. J.C. Willke, *Handbook on Abortion* (Cincinnati: Hiltz Publishing Co., 1972), p. 66.

[26]"Public Policy on Reproductive Choices," adapted from *Public Policy and Abortion,* Roberta Francis, New Jersey League of Women Voters, 1982, p. 3.

[27]Chambers, *op. cit,* p. 248.

[28]*Planned Parenthood versus Danforth,* 1976.

[29]Melody Green, "The Questions Most People Ask About Abortion" (Lindale, TX: Last Days Ministries, 1981).

[30]Ronald Reagan, *Abortion and the Conscience of the Nation* (New York: Thomas Nelson Publishers, 1984), p. 16.

[31]Willke, *op. cit,* p. 127. The fact that this baby was aborted alive and remained alive through transport from clinic to lab,

makes him viable. But laws are such that the spokesman for the clinic could (in 1970) legally say, "The position is quite clear. A fetus has to be 28 weeks to become legally viable [in England]. Earlier than that it is so much garbage" (quoted in Willke).

[32]C. Everett Koop, "A Physician Looks at Abortion," *Thou Shalt Not Kill,* ed. Richard L. Ganz (New Rochelle, NY: Arlington House, 1978), p. 22.

[33]Olga Fairfax, "101 Uses for a Dead (or Alive) Baby," *About Issues* (January 1984), pp. 4–8.

[34]*Ibid.,* p. 8.

[35]*Ibid.,* p. 6.

[36]Dwight J. Ingle, *Who Should Have Children?* (New York: Bobbs-Merrill Co., 1973), p. 116.

[37]Reagan, *op. cit.,* p. 38.

[38]Linda Bird Francke, *Ambivalence of Abortion* (New York: Random House, 1978), p. 255.

[39]Walter Barnett, *Sexual Freedom and the Constitution* (Albuquerque, NM: University of New Mexico Press, 1973), pp. 52–53.

[40]Group for the Advancement of Psychiatry, ed., *Humane Reproduction* (New York: Charles Scribner's Sons, 1973), p. 97.

[41]"Abortion and the Law," *Newsweek* (March 3, 1975), p. 23.

[42]Steven Waterhouse, "A Biblical Inquiry into the Value of the Unborn," Master's thesis, Capital Bible Seminary, 1982.

[43]Susan T. Foh, "Abortion and Women's Lib," *Thou Shalt Not Kill,* ed. Richard L. Ganz (New Rochelle, NY: Arlington House, 1978), p. 187.

[44]Paul Marx, "Contraception, the Gateway to Abortion," *About Issues* (November 1983), p. 20.

[45]Foh, *op. cit.,* p. 160.

[46]*Ibid.,* p. 150.

[47]*Ibid.,* p. 152.

[48]Group for the Advancement of Psychiatry, *op. cit.,* p. 43.

[49]"Feminists Against Abortion?" *Christianity Today* (April 22, 1983), p. 35.

Chapter 5—Acquiescently Aborted

[1]Magda Denes, *In Necessity and Sorrow* (New York: Basic Books, Inc., 1976), p. 265.

[2]C. Everett Koop, "A Physician Looks at Abortion," *Thou Shalt Not Kill,* ed. Richard L. Ganz (New Rochelle, NY: Arlington House, 1978), p. 18.

[3]Deborah W. Huff, "WEBA: Voice of Experience Relates Horror of Abortion."

[4]David Granfield, *The Abortion Decision* (Garden City, NY: Doubleday & Co., 1969), p. 43.

[5]R.F.R. Gardner, *Abortion: The Personal Dilemma* (Grand Rapids: William B. Eerdmans, 1972), p. 238.

[6]In 1985 a Virginia physician was accused of intentionally performing "abortions" on *non*pregnant women.

[7]Jill Lessard in Huff, *op. cit.*

[8]Denes, *op. cit.,* p. 141.

[9]Personal testimony of Ila Ryan.

[10]Maria Corsaro and Carole Korzeniowsky, *A Woman's Guide to Safe Abortion* (New York: Holt, Rinehart, & Winston, 1983), p. 54.

[11]John Lippis, *The Challenge to Be "Pro Life"* (Santa Barbara, CA: Santa Barbara Pro Life Education, 1978), p. 8.

[12]Corsaro and Korzeniowsky, *op. cit,* pp. 54–56.

[13]Gardner, *op. cit,* p. 221.

[14]Dr. and Mrs. J.C. Willke, *Handbook on Abortion* (Cincinnati: Hiltz Publishing Co., 1972), p. 76.

[15]Paul Marx, *The Death Peddlers* (Collegeville, MN: St. John's University Press, 1971), p. 18.

[16]Lippis, *op. cit,* p. 2.

[17]Willke, *op. cit,* p. 72.

[18]Lippis, *op. cit,* p. 2.

[19]Gardner, *op. cit,* pp. 72–73.

[20]Granfield, *op. cit,* p. 43.

Chapter 6—Actions Analyzed

[1]Betty Benjamin, "The Case for Pro-Choice," *Should Abortions Be Permitted?* ed. David L. Bender (St. Paul, MN: Greenhaven Press, n.d.), p. 97.

[2]For an in-depth discussion of this topic, see Landrum Shettles and David Rorvik, *Rites of Life* (Grand Rapids: Zondervan, 1983).

[3]Dr. and Mrs. J.C. Willke, *Handbook on Abortion* (Cincinnati: Hiltz Publishing Co., 1972), p. 9.

[4]C.F. Keil and F. Delitzsch, *Commentary on the Old Testament,* vol. 8 (Grand Rapids: Eerdmans, n.d.), p. 39.

[5]Shettles and Rorvik, *op. cit,* p. 115.

[6]Dick Hafer, "I Know that We're a Throw-Away Society . . . But This Is Ridiculous!" (Lanham, MD: The Comics Commando, 1981), p. 10.

[7]Ronald Reagan, *Abortion and the Conscience of the Nation* (New York: Thomas Nelson Publishers, 1984), p. 21.

[8]Willke, *op. cit,* p. 10.

[9]Hafer, *op. cit,* p. 10.

[10]Shettles and Rorvik, *op. cit,* p. 56.

[11]Benjamin, *op. cit,* p. 97.

[12]Shettles and Rorvik, *op. cit,* p. 40.

[13]David Granfield, *The Abortion Decision* (Garden City, NY: Doubleday & Co., 1969), p. 40.

[14]John Lippis, *The Challenge to Be "Pro Life"* (Santa Barbara, CA: Santa Barbara Pro Life Education, 1978), p. 3.

[15]Clifford E. Bajema, *Abortion and the Meaning of Personhood* (Grand Rapids: Baker Books, 1974), p. 15.

[16]Joseph Henry Thayer, *A Greek English Lexicon of the New Testament* (Grand Rapids: Zondervan, n.d.), p. 105.

[17]Jean Stalker Garton, *Who Broke the Baby?* (Minneapolis: Bethany Fellowship, 1979), p. 41.

[18]Charles Caldwell Ryrie, *You Mean the Bible Teaches That . . .* (Chicago: Moody Press, 1974), p. 89.

[19]Lippis, *op. cit.,* p. 4.

[20]Bajema, *op. cit.,* p. 22.

[21]Bernard Nathanson with Richard Ostling, *Aborting America* (New York: Pinnacle Books, 1979), p. 69.

[22]Magda Denes, *In Necessity and Sorrow* (New York: Basic Books, Inc., 1976), p. 159.

[23]"Last Days Newsletter," vol. 7, no. 6 (Garden Valley, TX: Last Days Evangelical Association), p. 17.

[24]Norman Anderson, *Issues of Life and Death* (Downers Grove, IL: InterVarsity Press, 1976), p. 83.

[25]Bill Shade, *How to Commit Murder and Make It Legal* (York, PA: n.p., 1971), pp. 45–47.

[26]Hafer, *op. cit.,* p. 11.

[27]Shettles and Rorvik, *op. cit.,* p. 119.

[28]Melody Green, "The Questions Most People Ask About Abortion" (Lindale, TX: Last Days Ministries, 1981).

[29]Shettles and Rorvik, *op. cit.,* p. 119.

[30]See Ephesians 5:28-33.

[31]David Granfield, *The Abortion Decision* (Garden City, NY: Doubleday & Co., 1969), p. 25.

[32]Clifford E. Bajema, *Abortion and the Meaning of Personhood* (Grand Rapids: Baker Books, 1974), p. 18.

[33]Jean Stalker Garton, *Who Broke the Baby?* (Minneapolis: Bethany Fellowship, 1979), p. 26.

[34]Herbert Vander Lugt, *A Matter of Life and Death* (Grand Rapids: Radio Bible Class, 1981), pp. 24–25.

[35]Bajema, *op. cit.,* p. 3.

[36]Claire Chambers, *The Siecus Circle: A Humanist Revolution* (Belmont, MA: Western Islands, 1977), p. 249.

[37]Harold O. J. Brown, *Death Before Birth* (New York: Thomas Nelson Publishers, 1977), p. 60.

[38]It is a fact that the abuse of children which abortion was to eliminate has increased because people's regard for all life has diminished as abortion has come to be widely accepted.

[39]Garton, *op. cit,* p. 31.

[40]Vander Lugt, *op. cit,* p. 28.

[41]Group for the Advancement of Psychiatry, ed., *Humane Reproduction* (New York: Charles Scribner's Sons, 1973), p. 450.

[42]R.F.R. Gardner, *Abortion: The Personal Dilemma* (Grand Rapids: William B. Eerdmans, 1972), p. 175.

[43]National Abortion Rights Action League, "20 Myths About Abortion," *Should Abortion Be Permitted?* ed. David L. Bender (St. Paul, MN: Greenhaven Press, n.d.), p. 73.

[44]Interview with Olga Fairfax, President of Methodists for Life, September 1984.

[45]Melody Green, "The Questions Most People Ask About Abortion" (Lindale, TX: Last Days Ministries, 1981).

[46]Brown, *op. cit,* p. 32.

[47]Landrum Shettles and David Rorvik, *Rites of Life* (Grand Rapids: Zondervan, 1983), p. 102.

[48]Richard L. Ganz, "Psychology of Abortion: The Deception Exposed," *Thou Shalt Not Kill,* ed. Richard L. Ganz (New Rochelle, NY: Arlington House, 1978), p. 37.

[49]Paul Kurtz, ed., *Humanist Manifestos I and II* (Buffalo, NY: Prometheus Books, 1973), p. 10.

[50]*Ibid,* p. 17.

[51]Chambers, *op. cit,* p. 233.

[52]*Ibid.*

[53]Kurtz, *op. cit,* p. 18.

[54]Ganz, *op. cit,* p. 37.

[55]Garton, *op. cit,* p. 28.

[56]Janet Gallagher, "The Fetus and the Law: Whose Life Is It Anyway?" *Ms.* (September 1984), p. 135.

[57]Paul Marx, *The Death Peddlers* (Collegeville, MN: St. John's University Press, 1971), p. 39.

[58]Dwight J. Ingle, *Who Should Have Children?* (New York: Bobbs-Merrill Co., 1973), p. 113.

[59]David LaFontaine, "The Case for Pro Life," *Should Abortions Be Permitted?* ed. David L. Bender (St. Paul, MN: Greenhaven Press, n.d.), p. 87.

[60]Granfield, *op. cit,* p. 131.

[61]John Lippis, *The Challenge to Be "Pro Life"* (Santa Barbara, CA: Santa Barbara Pro Life Education, 1978), p. 13.

[62]Granfield, *op. cit,* p. 126.

Chapter 7—Accountability

[1]Nora Scott Kinzer, *Stress and the American Woman* (Garden City, NY: Anchor Press/Doubleday, 1979), p. 150.

[2]Paul Marx, *The Death Peddlers* (Collegeville, MN: St. John's University Press, 1971), p. 29.

[3]Harold O. J. Brown, *Death Before Birth* (New York: Thomas Nelson Publishers, 1977), pp. 53–54.

[4]*Ibid.,* p. 54.

[5]*Ibid.*

[6]Richard L. Ganz, "Psychology of Abortion: The Deception Exposed," *Thou Shalt Not Kill,* ed. Richard L. Ganz (New Rochelle, NY: Arlington House, 1978), p. 32.

[7]*Ibid.,* p. 33.

[8]Dr. and Mrs. J.C. Willke, *Handbook on Abortion* (Cincinnati: Hiltz Publishing Co., 1972), pp. 41–42.

[9]Ganz, *op. cit,* p. 34.

[10]*Ibid.,* p. 31.

[11]Judy Miles, "Love Letter to a Girl in Trouble," Book Fellowship, n.d., p. 5.

Chapter 9—Applying Atonement

[1]Charles L. Feinberg, *The Minor Prophets* (Chicago: Moody Press, 1951), p. 207.

[2]In biblical times, a man often took several wives, but a woman could have only one husband at a time.

[3]Mark Porter, "Just How Righteous Is Our Anger?" *Moody Monthly* (December 1983), p. 79.

[4]Jay E. Adams, "What Do You Do When Anger Gets the Upper Hand?" (Phillipsburg, NJ: Presbyterian & Reformed Publishing Co., 1975), pamphlet.

[5]Porter, *op. cit.,* p. 80.

[6]Bob George, "There's No Need to Be Depressed," *Moody Monthly* (Feb. 1982), p. 7.

[7]Jay E. Adams, "What Do You Do When You Become Depressed?" (Phillipsburg, NJ: Presbyterian & Reformed Publishing Co., 1975), pamphlet.

Chapter 10—Alone and Anonymous

[1]Jay E. Adams, "What Do You Do When Fear Overcomes You?" (Phillipsburg, NJ: Presbyterian & Reformed Publishing Co., 1975).

[2]Joseph Henry Thayer, *A Greek-English Lexicon of the New Testament* (Grand Rapids: Zondervan, n.d.), p. 400.

Chapter 11—Aching Associates

[1]Eugene Kennedy, *What a Modern Catholic Believes About Sex* (Chicago: Thomas Moore Press, 1971), p. 109.

[2]Philip G. Ney, "A Consideration of Abortion Survivors," *Child Psychiatry and Human Development,* vol. 13 (Spring 1983), p. 168.

Chapter 12—Achieving Abundant Living

[1]Personal testimony of Kathy Smith.

[2]Tom Constable, "Is Prayer Optional?" source unknown.

[3]John W. Peterson, "New Life!" 1963, John W. Peterson Music. Used by permission.

Dear Reader:

We would like to know your opinion of the book you've just read. Your ideas will help us as we strive to continue offering books that will satisfy your needs and interests.

Send your responses to: **Victor Books**
1825 College Avenue
Wheaton, IL 60187

What most influenced your decision to purchase
Abortion's Second Victim?

☐ Front Cover ☐ Price
☐ Title ☐ Length
☐ Author ☐ Subject
☐ Back cover material ☐ Other: _____

What did you like about this book?

☐ Helped me understand myself better ☐ Good reference tool
☐ Helped me understand others better ☐ It was easy to teach
☐ Helped me understand the Bible ☐ Author
☐ Helped me understand God

How was this book used?

☐ For my personal reading ☐ As a reference tool
☐ Studied it in a group situation ☐ Added to a church or
☐ Used it to teach a group   school library

Please indicate your level of interest in reading other Victor books
like this one.

☐ Very interested ☐ Not very interested
☐ Somewhat interested ☐ Not at all interested

Would you recommend this book to a friend? ☐ YES ☐ NO

Please indicate your age.

☐ Under 18 ☐ 25–34 ☐ 45–54
☐ 18–24 ☐ 35–44 ☐ 55 or over

Would you like to receive more information about Victor books? If so,
please fill in your name and address below:

NAME:_____

ADDRESS:_____

_____

Do you have additional comments or suggestions?